Sketches OF A *Season*

Sketches OF A *Season*

TEXT BY

CHRISTOPHER MARTIN-JENKINS

ILLUSTRATIONS BY

JACK RUSSELL

Lennard Publishing
1989

Lennard Publishing
a division of Lennard Books Ltd

Musterlin House
Jordan Hill Road
Oxford OX2 8DP

British Library Cataloguing-In-Publication Data
Martin-Jenkins, Christopher
Sketches of a Season
1. Cricket - Stories, anecdotes
I. Title II. Russell, Jack
796.35'8

ISBN 1 85291 073 9

Edited by Michael Leitch
Cover design by Pocknell & Co.
Printed and bound by The Bath Press

CONTENTS

JANUARY

Tuesday, January 17th

Delegates have already started to assemble in Britain for the meeting at Lord's next Monday and Tuesday of the International Cricket Conference. Upon its outcome depends the smooth running of international cricket. At the centre of the debate, as everyone now knows, is South Africa. Hitherto the question at ICC meetings has been whether or not cricket administrators should take political decisions: now it is a question of which political decision they should take.

In the past England, which means in this case the TCCB, have always argued that the Conference (originally the Imperial Cricket Conference and founded in 1909, ironically, by South Africa herself in conjunction with England and Australia) should have as its only goal the spread and well-being of cricket in the world. Over the years England has played by far the greatest role in this respect, especially in the days when MCC was the power in the land and when tours with a missionary purpose were undertaken all over the globe. So successful were they that 18 Associate member countries, ranging from Bermuda to Bangladesh and including what some might consider the unlikely cricketing nations of Denmark, Israel, Argentina and Papua New Guinea, will line up with the seven Test playing nations on Monday. The new Associates will have one vote each, the full members two.

This disparate collection meets as usual under the chairmanship of the MCC President who this year is a formidable man of very high repute, Field Marshall Lord Edwin Bramall. A former President of ICC tells me that they could not wish for a better chairman in the circumstances. 'He is the sort of man to whom 40 people representing 25 different nations sitting round one table will not present any problem. He is an able man of the world.'

The heat, however, will be not so much on the chair – for MCC in international terms plays the role not of a British body but of experienced arbiter – as on the two TCCB representatives, Raman Subba Row and Doug Insole. Respectively the chairmen of the Board's executive and international committees, they have advised the counties, who meet on Thursday to determine TCCB policy at the ICC meeting, that England can no longer defend their players' right to go to South Africa to play or coach in the winter months without disrupting international cricket to such an extent that several counties would go bankrupt.

It is disappointing that the TCCB should not have been able to come up with a resolution of its own.

Thursday, January 19th

Having released to the press last week the fact that the executive committee saw no alternative to accepting four year bans, the TCCB full meeting today would not allow their Chief Executive to tell the meeting anything at all about what the policy is going to be at the ICC meeting on South Africa. Presumably they do not wish to compromise the position of the delegates, Doug Insole and Raman Subba Row. One must assume they have been given a mandate to accept four year bans, but not longer ones, and I hope they have suggested that this will be the last possible concession in reaction to the political whims of Governments.

The meeting was at The Oval, with all the cricket correspondents and the rather daunting television crews in attendance. The vacuum left by the Board's singularly taciturn statement was filled very willingly and capably by Joe Pamensky and Ali Bacher from the South African Cricket Union. They had come over in what is bound to be a vain attempt to persuade the ICC not to ban players going to their country, but they were able to address the TCCB this afternoon, eloquently enough to gain an ovation. There was a nice little exchange between the two men when they told the press about it in The Oval's Long Room.

Pamensky: 'We were pleased to be given a standing ovation.'

Bacher: 'No, not a standing ovation.'

Pamensky: 'No, sorry, an ovation. We were standing, they were sitting.'

These are two sincere and determined upholders of cricket in South Africa and one can only admire their fortitude in the face of so many rebuffs.

Tuesday, January 24th

After years of trying, the International Cricket Conference at last reached a consensus on South Africa. After agreeing to an amnesty for all who have been there in the past, the 25 countries represented at the special meeting agreed to suspend from all international cricket for at least four years any cricketer over the age of 19 who goes to play or coach cricket in South Africa after April 1st. Players so penalised will be allowed to appeal to the ICC for reinstatement after four years, or three if they are under 19. If they go on a tour the penalty will be five years.

The scenes at Lord's were genuinely dramatic. I arrived there at four, having done a television interview en route for the *Six O'Clock News*, anticipating the above decision, which had been well telegraphed in advance. In the brightly lit Long Room, surely one of the most attractive rooms in England, a battery of cameras and a semi-circle of chairs awaited the five o'clock press conference. On cue the former Chief of the Defence Staff, Field Marshall Lord Bramall, grey-haired, firm-jawed and confident without being strutty, emerged from the Committee Room with Col. John Stephenson, MCC's unflappable Secretary, to make the historic announcement that the 'health, unity and continuity' of international cricket had been preserved. No wonder Nancy, the engaging and warm-hearted Irish lady who rules the Lord's kitchen, was dispensing champagne to the delgates; a mood of mixed relief and emotion was evident from all except perhaps the Indians and Pakistanis who had wanted longer bans (originally, anyway) and who had tried more than Australia and New Zealand to stage the next World Cup in 1992, yet had lost the vote.

The decision on South Africa, which England supported, in fact which was unanimous, will not guarantee the untroubled exchange of international teams in future because it may yet suit governments to make political points by objecting to the presence in a team of someone eligible under ICC's new rules, but there is much optimism that this will not be the case, based largely on soundings taken by the architect of this expedient solution, the Jamaican barrister and former West Indies opening batsman, Allan Rae.

The delegates, disappointingly to me, did not discuss at any length the possibility of constraining governments from scuppering future tours in the way that India and Pakistan sank England's planned tours this winter, by agreeing that if such action were to be taken in future the offending country would not be allowed to stage any Test cricket for four years. One of the basic points about the need for this sad restriction on the freedom of individual players is that Governments have proved more powerful than cricket boards. When England withdrew from Guyana in 1981 and the England B tour to Zimbabwe and Bangladesh was called off in 1985 it was not because the cricket boards wished it so but because the governments of those countries wanted to make gestures against apartheid. No-one knows how the political situation will develop in South Africa and whether such protests might be repeated regardless of ICC agreements. Nevertheless the decision yesterday has in theory enabled England to continue touring overseas with a guarantee that no-one selected by them will have been to play cricket in South Africa in the previous four years.

Wednesday, January 25th

If the agreement does not founder on another political rock, it may yet do so on a legal one.

The Freedom Association, whose chairman is the brave, intelligent and high minded Norris McWhirter, sadly an athlete not a cricketer, is apparently determined to attack the ICC ruling on the grounds that it intimidates and restrains the trade of professional cricketers. The ICC, on the other hand, took counsel from the most renowned barrister in England, Lord Alexander, who as Robert Alexander, QC gave them such an unholy hammering in the Packer case ten years ago.

It is so difficult to know where the moral argument begins in this case. Is it right to restrict the freedom of the individual just to keep the lucrative international cricket circus turning? Is that freedom as important as the fundamental freedom which is taken away from black and coloured South Africans at birth? You can only answer this, I think, by deciding whether the lot of the deprived in South Africa will in any way be altered by the decision taken yesterday.

It should be on the conscience of the delegates that the action they have taken will do nothing to discourage the policy of *apartheid*. The protests of Asian and West Indies cricket administrators have a hollow ring when they allow their players to play against South Africans in county cricket and when the West Indies Board cheerfully take 40 per cent of the profits of their players through an agreement with Mark McCormack's International Management Group, which has open contact with many sporting events in South Africa.

We all know that this agreement at Lord's was a purely expedient one which will have, I repeat, no direct influence on the Nationalist government of South Africa. What the South African Cricket Union has been doing, on the other hand, might have. Black community leaders and ANC members had given moral and practical support for the projects over the last two years which, it is claimed, have introduced the game to 68,000 black youngsters in the townships. The same leaders share the opinion of Dennis Brutus, the chairman of SANROC, hitherto an entirely uncompromising pressure group aiming to isolate South African sport entirely, that the time has come to encourage genuinely non-racial sporting associations in South Africa to return to international circuits. Brutus, however, is not in accord with other SANROC officials, notably the single-minded Sam Ramsamy, and, like the Emperor Caesar, his days may be numbered. *Et tu Ramsamy*?

It is difficult to be sure how many British professionals will now risk going to South Africa. Already this winter the number has been cut to about 50. One man who didn't risk it was Angus Fraser, the very promising Middlesex fast bowler, who had agreed to go last summer only to withdraw for fear of prejudicing his international future. Ironically the amnesty means he could have gone and picked up much valuable experience. The flow of coaches, many of whom have been used to teaching cricketers of all colours and to playing in racially mixed teams, will be cut significantly. From the British professional's viewpoint a valuable avenue for winter employment has been closed, subject to legal action on restraint of trade.

No other country offers as much in terms of playing experience and remuneration. For this reason some young cricketers with perhaps only distant hopes of Test selection will continue to go to South Africa and other senior players who have had enough of the wearying international circuit will be only too pleased to go to the Republic as coaches, to play for provincial sides, or to play for the invited international teams who are bound to be gathered in future by South African cricket chiefs determined to keep the game going at all costs. Those costs will certainly be considerable and Ali Bacher, the SACU's chief executive, has said how much he would prefer to spend the money on developing young players of all races.

Instead, the 'phones will be ringing before long to the likes of Graham Gooch and John Emburey and it is a fair bet that several men will prefer to spend next winter fuelling the enthusiasm for cricket in South Africa rather than evading bouncers in the Caribbean.

Monday, January 30th

There was news today of a victory for Australia in the fourth Test against the West Indies in Sydney which just might have significance for the forthcoming Ashes series. Yet it was in many ways an artificial victory, in the sense that it was so untypical of the modern Test match. There were no fewer than 279 overs of spin – this with the West Indies as one of the two teams! – and Allan Border, a left-arm spinner who might get a few overs a season as an afterthought to speed up the over rate in county cricket, took 11 for 96 in the match. Incredibly these are the best figures by a Test captain, apart from Arthur Gilligan and Fazal Mahmood, the green-eyed policeman from the Punjab.

It was a singular triumph for the gritty little terrier whose own batting (he made a most painstaking 75) along with a fighting hundred by Boon made sure that all the wickets he took with long hops and full tosses in the first innings were not wasted.

Downend Cricket Club – one time home of W.G. Grace and Allan Border

Australia at Sydney seem to be a different proposition from Australia anywhere else. This, of course, is because the pitch there takes spin. Not that Australia's spinners are anything exceptional, proved by the fact that Border was the most effective of the three who played in the match. Peter Taylor seems less inclined to give the ball air than he did when making a most successful first appearance against England two years ago and Peter Sleep has lost this place to Trevor Hohns, another experienced leg-spinning all-rounder who would never have got close to an Australian Test side in any era before 1970.

The Australian success only underlines that the West Indies are doubly vulnerable on turning wickets. Their batsmen, starved of practice against spin bowling, generally do not have the technique to cope with the unfamiliarity of playing a slow, spinning ball all day long, because of the obsession with fast bowling and the preparation of pitches to suit them, both in the Caribbean and also in England and Australia where they play so much of their cricket. By the same token there are now few spin bowlers of real talent or experience in the Caribbean. I remember suggesting to Jackie Hendriks early on the West Indies tour of England last season that they would regret not bringing one of the young spinners who *have* had their successes in domestic cricket in order to learn to bowl in different conditions in matches against the counties. He felt that none had done enough to earn a place and was no doubt expressing a general West Indian viewpoint when stressing that the emphasis on fast bowlers had served their Test team rather well.

Only in India and Pakistan (discounting Sri Lanka who play so little first-class cricket) do spinners get the chance to compete regularly on equal, or even favourable, terms with faster bowlers. A look at the most recent performances in Sydney of India and Pakistan is therefore instructive. Australia fielded three specialist spinners – Bright, Holland and Matthews – when India played there in January 1986. India scored 600 for four declared and their first three batsmen, Gavaskar, Srikkanth and Mohinder Amarnath made 172,

116 and 138 respectively. India came close to winning, their three spinners, Yadav, Sivaramakrishnan and Shastri all doing well, but Boon, who loves batting at Sydney, made a characteristically dogged 131 and put on 217 for the first wicket with Marsh, which used up enough time to insure against subsequent collapses.

It is rare enough for any one to beat the West Indies in any conditions, so Australians have every right to rejoice. Their fickle supporters should now turn up in larger numbers for the final Test at Adelaide starting on Friday on what is usually one of the best pitches for batting in the world. Another Australian win is extremely unlikely, but they would get a further psychological fillip if they could emerge with a draw, remembering that their challenge for the Ashes begins in Leeds in a little over four months' time.

The psychology of the game is sometimes underestimated. By all accounts the West Indies did not do themselves any sort of justice at Sydney, that admirable cricketer Desmond Haynes apart. In particular Richards had a bad match as both captain and batsman. I wonder whether, knowing the pitch was not going to suit his own bowlers and with the weight of history counting against his team, he really believed he could win? If he did not, I suspect he was temporarily suffering from the same complex of inferiority which has held England back against the West Indies themselves so often in recent years.

Finally, a gambler's prophesy: Gordon Greenidge has never scored a Test hundred in Australia. He failed in both innings at Sydney. What price Greenidge hundred at Adelaide? I asked this of Ron Pollard of Ladbroke's who offered me a rather stingy 8 to 1. Nevertheless, I took him on with £10.

FEBRUARY

Tuesday, February 7th

The Adelaide Test was as usual a high-scoring draw and Greenidge did not let me down, though he waited until the second innings!

Friday, February 17th

I arrived in Johannesburg, leaving behind a premature spring with almond already in blossom, crocuses and snowdrops everywhere and daffodils about to bloom, to find the High Veldt unseasonally awash. The talk was all of floods and waterlogged grounds.

Some people will think me wrong to come to South Africa at all. By attending the Centenary celebrations, along with 40 other journalists, and doing some broadcasts, they will say that I am giving succour to *apartheid.* I simply cannot see this. The reverse, indeed is true. It is in the interests of South African cricket to see the quickest possible end to *apartheid* and I am all in favour of giving succour to South African *cricket.* Along with the former England captain and MCC President George Mann, I was met at the airport by Dr Ali Bacher, whose missionary zeal has been the driving force behind the various schemes to take cricket into the black townships. I want to see these developments at first-hand, rather than condemning or praising them without experiencing them, as so many cricket pundits have.

I do not for a moment doubt Ali Bacher's sincerity. His mission is to raise the dignity of the Africans through cricket, to use the game as a bridge between communities currently isolated from each other residentially by law, to keep the game going here at all costs, and to get South Africa, one day, back into international cricket. His enemies would argue, usually from the ignorance of distance, that the latter is his sole objective. It may have been his main aim once upon a time, but he knows there will be no return until African politicians are in charge in

Pretoria. Bacher is a man who cares for people and truly treats the black man as his equal.

Already, ordering room service at my hotel, a Holiday Inn which looks much like its counterparts all over the world, I am reminded how many Africans *do* feel servile in the presence of a white man. History and the pernicious *apartheid* laws have made them so. How could it be otherwise when they have to come into the 'white' cities to work (nowadays for good wages) but then have to go back into their own areas at night?

I hated *apartheid* when I first came here in 1963 to play some cricket and I hate it now. On that trip I came close to being assaulted by a bus conductor when I insisted on offering my seat to a portly African lady and I immediately lost interest in a pretty white South African girl when she spoke with spitting disparagement of someone being 'only a filthy kaffir'.

Since then the pass laws have been abolished; particular jobs are no longer reserved for whites; many 'blacks' have become wealthy and some have even sent their sons to private schools, there to gain confidence, competence and prestige; mixed marriages have become permissible; so too black-owned businesses and houses. Though the South African Government remains frightened of the consequences of change, huge sums have been poured by enlightened businesses into black welfare projects like the Urban Foundation. But there is still a long, long way to go and the more that the South African economy is squeezed by sanctions and expensive bank loans, the harder it is for these welfare projects to flourish.

It is just the same with cricket. Now the flow of coaches from overseas has been cut off, it will be that much harder for African cricketers.

Saturday, February 18th

Despite still cloudy weather and a ground which was completely waterlogged in places, Transvaal played and beat the Orange Free State today in the semi-final of the Nissan Shield, a 55-over contest. It was a disappointing game, despite fine innings by Fotheringham and Pienaar, played before a crowd of only two or three thousand, many of them schoolboys of various races, but it was interesting that the authorities insisted on the game getting started in conditions the over-fussy English umpires would never have considered remotely fit.

Sunday, February 19th

My admiration for Ali Bacher increased today when he asked me to share an informal barbecue lunch with some of his family at the house of their friends, Harry and Rosemary Phillips. Like the Bachers, Ali and Shira, they are Jews and they welcomed me generously and naturally into their circle. We talked politics freely and their opinions are every bit as liberal as my own. Harry is a General Practitioner who studied medicine with Ali Bacher. His son, Lawrence, who was away playing for the Wanderers Under-16 side, is apparently a quite outstanding young cricketer. So, too, is Bacher junior, David, a charming 14-year-old whose enthusiasm for cricket was evident from every word and gesture (practising his strokes with a knife and fork). He plays in the same school side as Graeme Pollock's son Anthony, who is apparently almost as prodigious a talent as his father. It is sad to think that they will probably never have the chance to represent their country in official Test matches.

The best indication of Bacher's sincerity in his drive to bring cricket to the blacks was not so much the fact that he had been in his office at six o'clock on a Sunday morning, or that the previous day he had arranged nets at the once very exclusive Wanderers Club for some keen youngsters from Soweto who had walked all the way – more than eight miles (Bacher gave them their bus-fare back) – to ask for more equipment, but a remark by young David quoted to me by his mother: 'Daddy, if I paint my face black will you come and watch ME playing cricket for a change?'

Any analysis of South African affairs by a visitor must be tackled with an awareness that much of South African life is unseen by someone staying in a big hotel in Johannesburg. It is so easy to be lulled by the feeling of affluence all around the tree-lined streets and to forget that the country is currently in an official 'state of emergency' with political prisoners being detained without trial, and press, radio and television all censored while the country's future is seriously threatened by economic sanctions and the drain of well qualified young men seeking a safer future overseas and an escape from compulsory military service. All this goes on at a time when many black leaders believe that violence is still a more likely means of achieving black majority rule than gradual evolution towards that goal through the creation of a wealthy, well-educated black middle-class.

It is easy, also, to overlook history and to remember that South Africa has only existed as a Union since 1910, its three main population groups still as much at odds with each other as they were then: the Afrikaners, many of whom still believe in a God-given right to 'their' land and a God-given superiority; the British commercial group who first exploited the country's huge mineral wealth and had little in common with either the Afrikaners or the natives; and the indigenous blacks, made up of several different tribes, who have always been kept outside the political system, with no votes and few rights.

That said, there has been much done to encourage evolution rather than revolution: abolition of some of the nastiest laws; a blind eye turned by the Government to 'grey' areas where different colours live in the same streets; positive discrimination for blacks in universities and in industry (the marketing manager of South African Breweries, Peter Savery, told me yesterday that his company now has 46 per cent blacks amongst its salaried workers and that the target was 50 per cent by next year), and, at the grass roots (or should one say 'in the dusty streets'), dedicated hard work by liberal people to ensure that whatever radical leaders from either side may say, charity begins at home.

Monday, February 20th

I saw for myself today some of the early fruits of the recent drive to take cricket into the black townships. I travelled to Johannesburg's Northern Suburbs with a representative Under 15 team from the Alexandra township in a mini-bus driven by one of the Southern African Cricket Union's voluntary coaches, John Jefferies. An ebullient ex-serviceman in his sixties, he has obviously earned the respect and affection of the keen young African cricketers. Today he made one of the best players twelfth man as a punishment for failing to turn up for a match the other day because it was raining. The boy was momentarily downcast but was soon singing rhythmic, harmonic songs with the rest of the team as we sped along a tree-lined freeway to Bryanston. 'Well done for taking it like a man,' said Jefferies before the game. 'You will definitely be playing in our last two matches.'

The boys have been beaten only twice this season in their matches against mainly white school teams. They lost to the mixed-race independent (fee-paying) boys' school, St John's, a school with a great cricket tradition and also to Park Town, a State-financed all-white school for boys aged 13 to 18. The rest of the games, however, have been won or drawn and today was to be no exception.

Bryanston, like Park Town, is an all-white school, loftily set in a pleasant, almost rural northern suburb with long views across extensive playing fields. They need the space, because there are over 1000 pupils, girls slightly outnumbering boys. I asked the headmaster Roy Paige, a slim, tanned, chain-smoking, conscientious 50-year-old, if he would like to have a mixture of races. 'Yes,' he replied unequivocally, 'and it will come. When the Group areas act goes, as it must, we'll take in any pupils from this area. Attitudes are changing so fast.' He pointed across the trees to the north: 'I live over there and a new black development is going up next door to us. Once it would have been a problem. Now it isn't. Someone asked me to sign a petition of complaint on the grounds that our property prices would fall. I told them, "no ways man, it's got to happen".'

Paige told me that it had once required a major bureaucratic effort to arrange a match like this. Now it is accepted as entirely normal and the boys react completely naturally to one another. If there was any feeling of inferiority on the part of the Africans - I noticed, for example, that the African captain didn't look his opposite number in the eyes when they shook hands before the toss - it struck me as being little different from what a state school team in England might feel when playing in the unfamiliar grandeur of a big public school. At any rate, cricket is building the confidence of the young Africans, and there was to be no doubt in this game about which side was the inferior one!

The Alexandra boys lost the toss and found themselves fielding on an outfield of coarse grass, thick from the recent rain. The pitch, hard sand covered by matting, played truly but the two opening bowlers, Peace and Andries, were immediately impressive, remarkably so for boys who, like the whole team, had only been playing cricket for 17 months. Peace is tall, slim and very fast for a 14 year old; a little erratic as yet but he has already learned to bowl an occasional slower ball and Ali Bacher told me later that he is doing well on Saturdays for one of Johannesburg's stronger club sides. His opening partner, Andries, impressed me even more. A gentle, loping run prefaced a lissome, outswinger's action and, like many young West Indians, he generated pace from natural rhythm. In his eight-over spell he knocked the stumps over four times at a cost of only 17 runs. Peace got a couple of wickets before giving way to Michael, who bowled flighty leg-spinners and soon whistled through the last three batsmen. Bryanston, by no means without talent themselves but with five more years of cricketing experience per boy, were all out for 40. After tea the Alexandra boys had moments of disappointment but they won by five wickets.

John Jefferies, justly proud of his charges, called in on Dr Bacher on the way home to give him the good news. Bacher had some in return: an all Afrikans school, Randburg High, had agreed to play a match next month.

Tuesday, February 21st

Two even better cricketers are emerging in Alexandra's Under 14 side. Walter Masemola and Billy Mabena are cousins whose mothers are twin sisters who came originally from Malawi.

There have been some promising African cricketers in the past, notably in Cape Province where John Passmore has been encouraging them for years and where his stadium at Langa has the best cricketing facilities in any of the townships. Most in the past have drifted away from the game after their schooldays, either distracted by the need to work or discouraged by coloured politicians still adhering to the slogan 'no normal sport in an abnormal society'. But the recent explosion of cricketing interest is different, actively encouraged as it is by African schoolteachers and community leaders. Every Saturday now the keenest young cricketers from the townships around Johannesburg swarm into the once ultra-exclusive Wanderers Club expecting to play either in mixed-race club games or at least in the beautifully kept nets.

'They are demanding cricket,' said Dr Bacher, 'and we cannot let them down.'

I saw Robin Thorne, a former medium pace swing bowler for Border and a retired executive with Barclays before the bank decided to pull out of South Africa, in action with his boys in the nets today. He was helped by John Jefferies, two Afrikaner coaches and one of the young Alexandra teachers, Rani Mtetra, who now plays cricket himself for a teachers' team.

Another schoolmaster, Edwin Mmatli, who is chairman of the Alexandra Primary Schools Sports Association, kept a fatherly eye on things for a while. Cricket, he said, 'has done much for the confidence of the boys. Before, it was a white sport. Now that it is played by blacks the mixing is doing much for relations between the two groups. The coaches are white and the boys have to play against whites. They then discover that they are all human beings.'

The net facilities were poor and the area distinctly seedy, despite the cheerful atmosphere. There were five concrete net pitches, but only three could be used because of the recent rain.

I pointed out to Edwin Mmatli that many people outside South Africa claimed that there were ulterior motives on the part of those teaching cricket to the Africans. I was politely rebuffed:

'That is not the case. They should come down and see for themselves. I cannot blame them because no good news leaves South Africa and reaches the outside world. But I can tell you that this has not been forced on us. If it had been forced I personally would not be here. This is a sport and the children love it. It is because of the love of the game that they play it. If there was political resistence within the township they would not have allowed these whites to come here. It is played at will and voluntarily.'

He added that his own interest had flowed from the visit of the 'rebel' West Indians. 'The fact that black people also played this sport was a surprise. Now, after only 17 months, we have a boy from this area going to the P.G. Wood representative team in Port Elizabeth.'

That boy was Peace. Was it just coincidence that two of the three other black boys chosen on merit from throughout Transvaal for the P.G. Wood week were called Justice and Harmony?

Thursday, February 23rd

Off to another township today, with the former Transvaal and North Transvaal cricketer Francois Weideman, a quiet, friendly young man now fully employed by the SACU to co-ordinate schemes in the townships around Pretoria. No doubt Ali Bacher, resourceful as he is, was keen to have an Afrikaner involved.

Weideman says his own motives are a desire to give something back to cricket and a strong feeling that he is doing something socially worthwhile. There is no doubt about that. We travelled on yet another humid, cloudy day through handsome sweeping country to Attridgeville, a community on the outskirts of Pretoria which is beautifully kept by its citizens. Each little house seemed to have its own well tended garden. Apparently the City Council offer prizes for the best kept properties.

We went to one of four primary schools in the town in which cricket has taken firm hold, inspired by a delightful old enthusiast called Charles who used to go to watch the touring sides as far back as the 1950s and talks with reverence of 'Mr Denis Compton', rolling the name slowly off his tongue. He was overjoyed when the SACU started sending coaches to the school and immediately got involved. His ambition, he says, is to see one of his boys becoming 'a Springbok'.

Neatly attired in white shirts and shorts supplied by the mini-cricket sponsors, the boys, some thirty eleven-year olds, had a lively, orderly net practice under Charles's enthusiastic eye. Most of the boys had a good idea of bowling – these were the most promising of the thousands who were first introduced to soft-balled mini-cricket – although their batting looked in one or two cases to be over-coached and therefore a little inhibited. Nevertheless there was obvious native talent, and it was even more evident when they had a game of mini cricket on the bumpy-stoned school yard. Their fielding was fearless and good.

Before leaving I was given tea by the headmaster and a school inspector and we had a fascinating political talk. They are staunch Christians, firmly against all boycotts and sanctions ('Sanctions lead to unemployment and that puts youngsters on the streets needing to find bad ways of making a living') and the headmaster at least seems convinced that things will change more quickly now that the leader (P.W. Botha) is ill and having to relinquish some of his power.

I mentioned that boycotts and sanctions would continue if respected men like Bishop Tutu continued to support them. 'Tutu is a priest not a politician', was the reply. 'If people like Tambo could come back now

I am sure he would be amazed to see how much better the townships are.'

Tambo, of course, is banned, like so many ANC leaders. The next stage will not come until the Government starts to encourage them back. But it seems very unlikely they will take that gamble especially in the face of growing conservative opposition to any more concessions. And two of the apartheid pillars are still standing - the classification of people by colour and their enforced residence in specified areas.

Friday, February 24th

I spoke last night at a dinner at The Wanderers in honour of the 14 surviving South African Test umpires. Many legends of the cricket field were there and I met for the first time Clive Van Ryneveld, Eric Rowan and Roy Maclean. Curiously enough, two octogenarian umpires had actually stood in matches in which I played: Del Collins, who once gave Bruce Mitchell out for 99 against England after consulting with the other umpire - his brother (a unique achievement for brothers) and Farley Paine whom I had accidentally knocked flying when moving from mid-wicket to square-leg to field the first ball of a match five years ago!

Saturday, February 25th

One-day cricket at its best can be a marvellous game and the South African cricket community of all colours was buzzing with excitement this evening after a thrilling first-leg of the Nissan Shield Final, the equivalent of our NatWest Trophy. In the beautiful setting of Newlands which remains, in my view, easily the prettiest ground on which Test cricket has been played, Western Province beat Transvaal by four wickets with two balls in hand. Daryl Cullinan, a brilliant 21-year-old right-hander who would strengthen any county team, and Eric Simons were the two younger cricketers to catch my eye. Simons is a tall, well balanced fast bowler who took a superb catch off his own bowling to dismiss Clive Rice during Transvaal's final charge towards 216-6 in their 51 overs (the game was reduced by eight overs because of early rain) and he also batted well.

The atmosphere at Newlands, which combines Adelaide's grandeur with Worcestershire's leafy charm, was just like that at any big match anywhere else in the world, be it Port of Spain, Perth or even Jack Russell's Bristol on one of its rare big occasions: sedate members of Western Province in the pavilion, men stripped to the waist to soak up the sun in the open stands under the oak and plane trees, and a seething mass of mainly coloured enthusiasts under the willows singing, chanting and dancing in support of the home side. All good clean fun at least until the last few balls when, to the annoyance of Jimmy Cook (who again batted well and will I'm sure do well for Somerset this year), about a hundred over eager spectators encroached over the boundary's edge.

Monday, February 27th

Having moved from Johannesburg to Cape Town, I have quickly become aware of differences in the cricket scene. Whereas in the Transvaal cricket is a relative novelty now being eagerly claimed by the Africans, here it has been played with enthusiasm and skill by the Indians and coloureds (as it has in Natal) for almost as long as the English.

It was from Cape Town that Basil D'Oliveira, already in his thirties, left for England after a whip-round by cricketers of all colours to pay his expenses. A decade later, when it had become clear, thanks to Peter Hain and David Sheppard and all the others who froze South African's brilliant Test team (Barlow, Procter, the Pollocks and all) out of world cricket, the more enlightened cricket administrators came tantalisingly close to genuine autonomy in cricket in this area. For years white cricket had been separately run by the SACA (Association) and 'coloured' cricket by the SACBOC, later the SACB (Board).

The main characters in the drama were the former Test captain Jack Cheetham, another white administrator, Boon Wallace, and two from the coloured and Indian community, Rashid Verachia and Hassan Howa. They formed the new non-racial SACU but when all seemed agreed after months of planning and debate Howa, a warm-hearted, very intelligent, mercurial man, refused to co-operate. Both sides accuse the other for this breakdown of relations in 1977, Howa's version being that Wallace had not trusted him because he had drawn up two sets of fixtures, one to include clubs of all colours, one for whites only in case the agreement failed.

In the event several coloured clubs did become members of the new SACU but as the politics of the anti-apartheid sports boycotters have hardened in the last 12 years, led by the SACOS (Council of Sport) only one of them has remained and thrived. This is Avendale which now runs 10 mixed-race teams from Under-10 to the senior team which, boosted by English professionals, has won the premier league. The club's chief inspiration has been the former Kent and England cricketer Bob Woolmer. He first came here in 1981 and has made it his life's work since to make the club something everyone can be proud of.

Avendale is situated in a huge open area on the edge of the coloured township of Athlone. Woolmer remembers that it was all a bit of a mess when he first came here:

'We had two concrete nets with uneven bounce; a pitch with no roller; good cricketers without any properly organised coaching. To be able to play professional cricket and coach seriously is almost impossible, so the second winter I came out here I made myself unavailable for Western Province and put everything I had got into developing this club.'

Woolmer married a South African girl and has settled here. He is viewed with tremendous respect by the coloureds but with a certain amount of suspicion, I sense, by the white cricket establishment. He was not, for example, given the responsibility of co-ordinating 'black' cricket development in the area by the Western Province Cricket Union, a job given instead to a non-cricketer. Woolmer wanted to have an office in the townships; instead the coaching schemes are run from the 'safety' of the wealthier white suburbs. Their patronage of African cricket here is genuine enough, but is still done at arm's length, largely no doubt from fear of the sometimes militant SACOS city politicians, who continue to refuse to co-operate even to the extent of refusing offers of better facilities and denying their schoolchildren the chance to be coached, play games with whites, or use the facilities of non-SACOS clubs. Their cry is still 'No normal sport in an abnormal society'. In the next few days I shall try to discover how they justify this when it is clear that non-racial sport has done so much to make society *more* normal. I gather SACOS themselves face hostility and obstruction from the Government's Education Department.

Avendale has developed, during the past eight years, marvellous facilities for its largely coloured membership through money raised by a philanthropic Jew, Mike Stakel (who has left the country now, apparently under a cloud). Woolmer himself has laid a superb turf pitch on the main ground (there are three in all) and extensive net pitches. Every now and again the nets are slashed and promising young cricketers are intimidated away from the club. There is still a long way to go.

To give just one example, the school next door to Avendale's playing fields has no ground of its own but the headmaster will not allow use of the Avendale fields, though they are willingly offered. If their boys play for the club they are banned from the school's soccer and athletics team. But Woolmer points out that by no means all is obstruction. The Athlone City Council actually owns Avendale and have generally been supportive, just as the African township nearby has given its blessing to the development of similarly excellent facilities at Langa, thanks to the marvellous work of John Passmore, the 'father of African cricket'. A major dinner is being held on Saturday to raise money for the further development of Langa and I am going to speak at it.

The Cape Town business community is confidently expected to rally round and support the new Passmore Trust.

Tuesday, February 28th

Prior to a delightful drive round the Cape Peninsula with Martin Young, the former Worcestershire and Gloucestershire batsman and for many years since a cricket commentator here – and a convivial evening round his bar later – I have a most interesting day in the company first of Jannie Momberg and then of Omar Henry.

Momberg is an Afrikaner from Stellenbosch, the quite beautiful university town in the wine growing area in the valley leading to the Hottentot Holland mountains which rise into a blue haze beyond the neat, green rows of vines. He is a heavily built retired wine farmer, a long-time supporter of the Nationalist party but now engaged with Dennis Worrell and other white politicians in forming the opposition Democratic Party.

Momberg is clear that all the *apartheid* laws have to be abolished. There is no such thing, he says, as reforming *apartheid*. 'You are either pregnant or not; you cannot be half pregnant.' He has changed political parties out of conviction, not convenience. 'Once you leave the inner circles you have done it for good,' he says. 'The Bruderbond disown you for ever.'

Though his political conversion may have come late - he will stand as MP for Seapoint in the election (which is thought to be imminent) - Momberg was in the vanguard of opening up white sport to all races in his roles as an athletics and cricket administrator. Boland, the cricketing area of which Stellenbosch is the centre, has been fielding coloured players for many years and was the first to do so.

Omar Henry is one of them. Almost jockey-sized, a Moslem, he is a left-arm orthodox spin bowler and basman who was the only coloured man good enough to get into the 'Springbok' side against the unofficial Australian touring teams a few seasons ago. He risked ostracism and had to resist threats on his life and property when he finally decided to play in SACU rather than SACOS cricket. 'They were telling me I could not play with white cricketers at Kingsmead even though I was staying with them on the beach at Durban. I crossed to the so-called white side for myself, to further my cricket career, and also because I believed it would help to break down *apartheid.*'

Henry continues to be employed by the Scottish Cricket Union as professional and has had a successful season with Boland in the Castle Bowl and with the Impalas (a grouping of three 'B' provinces) in the one-day competitions, the Nissan Shield and the Benson and Hedges. (He has also had a benefit this year, with Momberg its chief inspiration.)

He was born in Stellenbosch and remembers how he used to watch cricket at Newlands, 20 miles away in Cape Town, as a boy in an area then designated for coloureds only. Basil D'Oliveira told him he could 'make it' as a professional cricketer but refused to believe he would ever be allowed to play cricket at Newlands. Officially treated with disdain by SACOS, he was loudly appreciated by his fellow coloureds in their favoured position under the willows at Newlands when I saw him have an outstanding all round match for the Impalas against Western Province.

MARCH

Wednesday, March 1st

I went today to speak to the Secretary and Vice-President of SACOS, the rallying point in sporting circles for all opposition to apartheid and the Government which invented it and which still supervises and sustains it. They were uncompromisingly rigid in their views but impressive as men of deep conviction in any field always are.

Driving to the heart of Athlone and walking into the offices of the solicitor Joe Ebrahim (a very pale-skinned, officially 'coloured', studious, lucid Moslem of about 45) I felt, if not fearful, at least apprehensive. Perhaps this was partly because Frank Brache, who had kindly shepherded me to the right place, parted with the words, 'Good luck, Chris, you're on your own now.'

The fundamental message to come from our meeting was that SACOS will not co-operate with other sporting organisations in South Africa, however enlightened or however truly non-racial, until the Government has lost power and *apartheid* has been totally disbanded.

Colin Clarke, the SACOS secretary, is a taut, energetic coloured Christian of perhaps 30, with an almost fanatical zeal in his eyes. He smoked in Ebrahim's office, despite a sign saying 'Thank you for not smoking.' He is bitter in his condemnation of the Government, angry that so many good coloured sportsmen for some hundred years have wasted their sweetness (and their sweat) on the desert air. He clearly mistrusts most establishment whites, including those from the South African Cricket Union.

Ebrahim says that the actions of the SACU have not demonstrated their professed abhorrence of *apartheid*. By threatening further rebel tours, he says, they have ignored the United Nations moratorium on tours to South Africa. 'SACU's motives are of self-preservation and maintaining their position of dominance in cricket in South Africa. They have not given recognition to cricket organised by SACOS.'

He refers to SACU as a 'racialist organisation' despite their coaching schemes in the townships because, unlike SACOS, they are still prepared to recognise and work with the government. To allegations that SACOS intimidate cricketers who co-operate with the SACU he says: 'Once an individual chooses to go on a particular course of conduct, that individual must accept that others have a right to decide whether to associate with him. Omar Henry and others have a right to go and play for SACU in the same way that we don't want to associate with him or have him as a member.'

I pointed out that the school next to Avendale does not allow its pupils to use the club's excellent facilities. He counters: 'We are past the stage where we want to accept handouts and better facilities. If our members are to participate it has to be under the aegis of the South African Council on Sport, because sport has been used in the past for political purposes by the Government. Those who have been involved in racialist sport have acquiesced. We do not see the likes of the SACU as being sincere.' He compares them with those who gave tacit approval to the Third Reich in Germany in the 1930s.

Only when the South African Government concedes a universal franchise will SACOS accept 'normal sport' or support South Africa's re-entry into international sport. For the 'coloured' South African Cricket Board (which operates as an arm of SACOS) to join hands with the SACU, the latter would, in the words of Joe Ebrahim, of SACOS, first 'have to state in unequivocal terms its opposition to *apartheid*; second to see that its members don't participate in Government – no consultation with Government ministers, no members who are MPs or Government officers; thirdly to refuse to recognise the Government; fourthly to accept that SACOS must take over the organisation of all cricket; fifthly to understand that they won't get back into international sport until all other codes of sport, as well as cricket, have become totally integrated.'

Ebrahim says he has 'serious doubts' about cricket being used as a medium to change and improve South African society and to improve the status of the dispossessed of South Africa, despite the fact that many African community leaders have accepted this idea and co-operated willingly in the development of cricket in the townships. 'So long as one of my brothers is enslaved,' he says, 'all of us are enslaved.'

He denies that this is a power struggle between Africans on one hand and 'Coloureds' and Indians on the other; or between Moslems and Christians; or between the Cricket Union and the Cricket Board. But his fundemental stand, and that of SACOS, is that sporting change must be subject to political change. Not until there is a 'reunification of South Africa and a universal franchise' will there be totally open sport.

Sunday, March 5th

In Cape Town, as Avendale and Langa prove, it has been different for some time, although progress is slow and it needed the launching of the John Passmore Trust at a big dinner on Saturday to ensure that their work would continue. Passmore looked on benignly as his Langa team took on an International Wanderers team including such players as Dennis Amiss, Graeme McKenzie, Ashley Mallett and Keith Fletcher, at the pleasant, spacious Langa ground where the view of Table Mountain is spoilt only by the power station whose smelly emissions reach the nose unmistakably on the stiff breeze which blows almost all the time.

Although SACOS will probably win the political battle within sport, at least until the ANC dictate otherwise, young people of all colours are increasingly mixing through the medium of cricket. When the last *apartheid* law goes, the game will be seen to have played an honourable part in creating a more just society.

Tuesday, March 14th

Twenty-one Test captains were gathered in Port Elizabeth at the weekend to watch the final of the Currie Cup, the main domestic competition which will itself be 100 years old by next year. They watched a game which in standard was very close to that of the County Championship in England or the Sheffield Shield in Australia. The West Indian equivalent, now sponsored by Red Stripe, is different in character because of all the genuinely fast bowlers but that could very well change in time if the promising young African bowlers now being developed here are not just part of a mirage in a desert. If, as everyone hopes, the Africans do begin to come to the fore in cricket run by the SACU, it is unlikely that we shall see, as we have at St George's Park, the majority of overs being bowled by spinners.

There are 13 players with international experience in the Transvaal and Eastern Province sides and the first day was enlivened by a century of characteristic charm and elegance by that most gentlemanly of modern cricketers, Ken McEwan. His innings of 191 contained many of the drives and square and late cuts which marked his consistently successful batting for Essex for many years. This was his 76th hundred. Amongst those who suffered at his hands were Clive Rice and Neal Radford. The Bajan fast bowler Rod Estwick, who has had a good season hitherto, was left out of the side to accommodate a second Transvaal spinner on a dry pitch but Greg Thomas of England (and Wales) and Rod McCurdy of Australia ensured a cosmopolitan flavour to a match watched by considerable crowds. Eastern Province, having made 562 a bit too slowly, finally wheedled out Transvaal twice, winning a tense game which, with Rice batting over eight hours in all, went into the final hour.

This worthy match was something of a relief to the SACU, not just because this was the climax of their centenary celebrations, but also because the trend here has followed that almost everywhere else: big crowds for one-day matches, extremely choosy ones for the two-innings game. The Currie Cup Final was in fact played over five days, to try to ensure a fair result and to keep South African players in tune with the 'Test' cricket which no doubt they will be playing again next season against an imported team, from somewhere, almost certainly Britain.

Wednesday, March 15th

My final day in South Africa was in many ways the most inspiring.

East London is the capital of Border, a small and old fashioned port with a huge, relatively well spaced out neighbouring township, Mdantsane. Here an enthusiastic sports organiser, Thako May, a friendly, positive woman who has given heart and soul to the cricket programme from its inception, has worked in harness with the Border Cricket Union's full-time organiser of township cricket, Greg Hayes. A former Border and Sussex second eleven all-rounder from the same school at Queenstown as Tony Greig and Ken McEwan, Hayes relishes his task. He was born and bred in the Ciskei, now an 'independent' homeland, and he speaks fluent Xhosa, the 'clickety click' language which takes years to master if you have not been brought up with it.

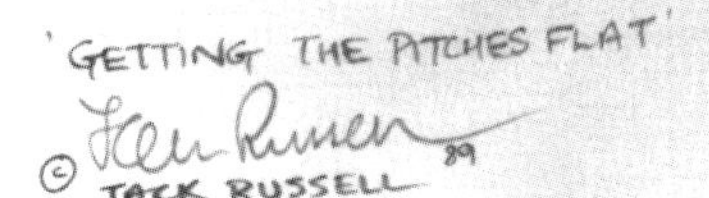

In Mdantsane there is a large field with an unkempt outfield but a firm mud pitch kept in good order by a heavy roller. Such is the talent of the boys from the many primary and high schools around here that Mrs May says she wants to challenge Alexandra, the place which has got all the publicity. 'We are just as good,' she says with an engaging chuckle. It had rained the day I visited so there was no-one about to prove her point but I do not doubt it having earlier been with Hayes into the beautiful hill country of the Ciskei to see school after school where in primitive villages cricket has taken root.

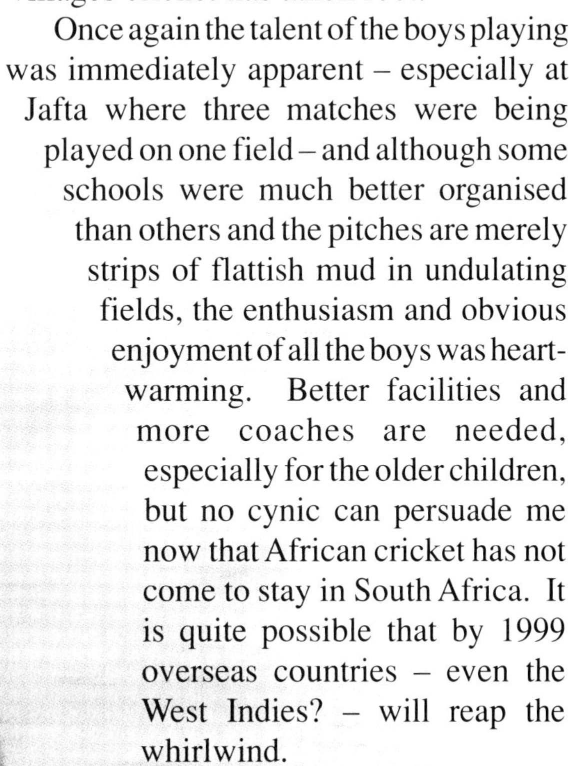

Once again the talent of the boys playing was immediately apparent – especially at Jafta where three matches were being played on one field – and although some schools were much better organised than others and the pitches are merely strips of flattish mud in undulating fields, the enthusiasm and obvious enjoyment of all the boys was heart-warming. Better facilities and more coaches are needed, especially for the older children, but no cynic can persuade me now that African cricket has not come to stay in South Africa. It is quite possible that by 1999 overseas countries – even the West Indies? – will reap the whirlwind.

The SACU is anxious to stress its financial independence of Government but if the Nationalist Government wishes to demonstrate its support for cricket development it should spend far more generously than before on the provision of playing fields for the township schools. Physical education should be as important as mental and spiritual, and the provision of proper sporting facilities for the young is almost as vital as the need to abolish the remaining *apartheid* laws themselves.

APRIL

Monday, April 17th

The last first-class match I watched last season was dominated by Graeme Hick, who made 197 on a difficult wicket at Worcester, setting up the victory which won the Championship. The first match of the 1989 English season was also essentially a *tour de force* by Hick. On the Saturday in sunny, if cool, spring weather, with the trees at the Nursery End not yet in leaf, he scored the first 35 of his eventual 173 not out. Playing for MCC, Lawrence, Agnew, Medlycott and, especially, Fraser all bowled well at him but he played and missed much less often than anyone else and he hit every bad ball for four. Robin Smith told me that during Sunday's play, whilst Hick was making 102 between lunch and tea, Chris Cowdrey once discomforted Hick with a ball which popped unexpectedly, perhaps off a small pebble. As he walked back Cowdrey, eager to claim the credit, remarked to Smith from the side of his mouth: 'I saw him rocking onto the front foot.'

To appreciate this you need to know Cowdrey's sense of humour and the unlikelihood of a medium pacer like him *ever* intentionally discomforting a genius like Hick with a bouncer.

Genius? Don't you doubt it. He is not 23 years old until next month and he has just scored his 41st hundred in first-class cricket, one more than David Gower has got in 349 more innings – and Mike Brearley rightly called David Gower 'a minor genius'. Hick has scored a hundred every third time he has gone to the wicket in the last two years. Overall, so far, he has a hundred in one out of every 4.8 innings. Even this is second only to Bradman. In the last 12 months he has scored, here and in New Zealand, 16 centuries and 3,941 runs at an average of 82. All by dint of fitness, concentration, a very quick eye and a simple, pure method.

Worcestershire would have declared anyway but we saw no-one scoring anything today because it rained all morning and the ground was too wet afterwards. So it was a day for conversation and time-filling reminiscences. In the kitchen Nancy was her usual generous self with coffee and tea, sandwiches and biscuits. MCC had found a sponsor –

Bass the brewers – for their two main matches of this and future seasons and were administering largesse from the President's Box in the Tavern stand. The lunch menu was salmon and *summer* pudding! Once play had been called off on a grey, very cold afternoon, Mick Hunt and his team got to work with mowers and rollers as the little blue tractor went buzzing back and forth amongst the white tarpaulins. One can't help feeling that groundsmen are the same the world over – much happier when there is no cricket and no crowd and they can get on with their business unmolested. They are supreme pessimists, like those who eat prunes with their All-Bran.

Amongst conversations I had during the day were interesting ones on the inevitable subject of South Africa with Don Kenyon and, the original catalyst, Basil D'Oliveira; and another with Trevor Bailey who mentioned in passing that all the fast left-arm bowlers before the war used to bowl *round* the wicket. It was something I had not really thought about before although I knew that Bill Voce, George Hirst and Nobby Clark were amongst those who had done so. I cannot think of any modern counterpart. The angle must greatly have reduced the chances of an lbw which wins a modern left-arm over merchant like J.K. Lever so many of his wickets.

Tuesday, April 18th

Although there were good performances today at Lord's by Phil Newport, Ian Botham, who bowled 20 overs of gentle medium pace for one wicket and only 36 runs – not to mention taking two slip catches, one of them brilliant – and from John Carr, Robin Smith and Allan Lamb who all got fifties, the main talking point has been whether or not Graeme Hick will have to wait until 1993, rather than 1991, to play for England. This assumes, of course, that he doesn't now prefer to play for New Zealand, who would have him tomorrow, or Zimbabwe, who apply for Test status in July.

The decision revolves around whether the matches which Hick

played for Zimbabwe against the Young Australians and New South Wales between October 1985 and March 1986 were deemed to be first class. If they were not considered first-class at the time he played in them, he may yet qualify in 1991. In fact, statisticians are in no doubt that the matches were *always* considered first-class – before, during and after – but Hick himself said this evening that he had received assurances that playing for Zimbabwe would not affect his qualification for England.

It seems to me that since 1991 was the date on which Hick had his heart and eyes set on the basis of 'official' information, and even if the assurances given to him were mistaken, he *should* be allowed, for humanitarian and pragmatic reasons, to play for England then even if it means bending the rules on Thursday when the Registration committee will be meeting. If that sounds weak, there is always room for the exception which proves the rule. It would be folly for England to turn their back on such talent and such an exemplary character. You cannot, and should not be able to, become an 'Englishman' overnight but Hick is no different from any other immigrant and has made his commitment to England quite plain since 1986.

Monday, April 24th

I played my first two games of cricket this weekend, against Radley for MCC and the Free Foresters. The first game was won and the second lost, despite a rather undisciplined batting performance by the boys who know a little more now about the importance of playing every ball on its merits. One or two of them were kind enough to get out to me and I made a few runs, respectably enough, I hope, not to embarrass my watching elder son against whom I hope to be playing in the same fixtures next year. They are speaking well of his progress.

The weather on Saturday was chilly, with every now and then just a hint of sun lighting up the long, even, open playing fields of Radley. The trees were still in their earliest, most delicate shades of green but you could see the tracery of the branches through the leaves.

From time to time one hears the argument that the season should start later and end later; that September is invariably a better month than April. If it were my choice I would start in mid April and go on to the very end of September when heavier dews and shorter daylight hours tend to counter-balance the advantage of warmer temperatures. The meteorologists would tell us for certain, but I would guess that rainfall is more or less even between the two months.

Since, because of my job, spring and autumn tend to represent the 'high summer' of my own active cricket, I am naturally biased. One has to be keen in one's mid-forties to play through three hours of mizzling rain in a temperature little above freezing, as I cheerfully did this weekend. On Sunday we lost in near to pitch darkness by nine runs but, stiff and sore though I remain in back, legs and shoulder I look back on the experience as being wholly pleasurable. That is not to say, of course, that it would not have been even more fun on a golden summer's evening, but it certainly *is* to say that cricket can be played in most weather conditions – and enjoyed in them – if the will is there.

Beggars cannot be choosers. Thanks to the complete insensitivity of Examination Boards to the needs of young cricketers (and I am not jesting - cricket is, after all, a national game and part of our heritage), school and university players have no choice but to practise and play through April showers. Come June, even May in some cases, GCSE, A-levels or Tripos exams will have taken precedence over outswingers and cover-drives.

There is an occasional exception. One sometimes hears apocryphal stories of this nature but I really did sit next to a Cambridge cricket captain – he was already a West Indies Test cricketer – who wrote his name at the top of his History paper, sighed a few times as he vainly tried to make sense of any of the questions before, like a bemused batsman dancing blindly down the pitch to a leg-spinner he cannot read, he put away his pen and left the Examination Hall. Inevitably it was his last term at the University. (Since he had presided over a singularly unsuccessful University side, refusing to give a chance to one or two of us producing much better performances for the Crusaders, the second XI, I did not feel all that sorry for him, although he was a quiet, dignified and most likeable person. But that is another story.)

I was saddened to hear at Radley, where cricket has retained its proper place in the scheme of things without detriment to the exam performances of any of the pupils, that the school captain, an outstanding young cricketer who has played with distinction for Middlesex and England school sides, had not even been considered by Oxford despite the fact that, being only a few miles away from Radley, it was his 'natural' university. The cricket master, himself a former Oxford blue, had tried to explain to tutors at more than one College that young Mark Lowrey was not just a cricketer but also a worthy character who would probably get an A and a couple of Bs in his A-levels and would contribute usefully to several areas of university life. He received a very cold shoulder. Academic excellence alone, he was told, was all that mattered. One needs to look no further than this for an explanation of the decline of Oxford sport, although I really cannot believe that there is not a more enlightened view in some parts of that great University.

Happily Cambridge have in this particular case recognised that a good all-rounder can be as valuable as the potential gainer of a first-class degree and Lowrey will be accepted at Homerton College for a teaching degree if he gets some reasonable A-levels. In the course of time this promising off-spinner and opening batsman will no doubt win a blue and make a mark in other fields. Had Cambridge also chosen to eschew such talent, he would probably have been cheerfully accepted at Durham where cricket is given an extremely high priority. They have in residence this term a number of current and future county cricketers and their general stock as a university is all the higher for the sensible attitude they take towards sport. Have the Dons of other universities really forgotten what Wellington said about the winning of the Battle of Waterloo?

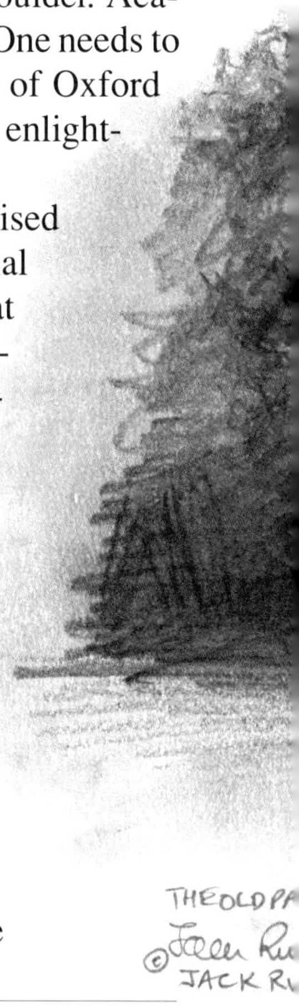

Helped by this chilly April weather neither Oxford nor Cambridge has yet lost a first-class match, so they have certainly got some good cricketers in residence whatever the intentions of the tutors for admission. As for the counties, David Gower made 228 on Saturday, his highest first-class score and a most heartening sign that he is in the mood to buckle down to his responsibilities. But with the weather spoiling several potentially good finishes only Worcestershire actually won, Hick getting 55 (not out) of the 126 they needed to beat Nottinghamshire. Essex were only two wickets short of beating Kent at Canterbury when rain prevented victory, and both Northamptonshire and Derbyshire came close to winning.

Hick was duly 'reprieved' by the Registration Committee of the TCCB Committee last Thursday (under the command of the Warden of Radley, Dennis Silk, incidentally). They gave a strange reason for their decision to confirm that he would be qualified for England in two years' time. They claimed that there had been doubt at

the time that the matches he played in England in 1985 and in Zimbabwe the following winter were first-class. It would have been simpler and more honest to invoke the clause that the regulations in question are ‘subject to the overriding discretion of the Board’. But it must be hard when sitting on these committees to see what those not responsible for the decision can often see more clearly. What matters is that they have come to the right conclusion, albeit by a circuitous route.

Tuesday, April 25th

Having written my strictures about the attitude of Oxbridge tutors towards sport in general and cricket in particular, the Combined Universities promptly produced a most efficient performance yesterday to overcome Surrey in a B and H zonal match. Significantly, however, the majority of the team was drawn from the other universities with James Boiling of Durham, the Young England off-spinner, producing a telling spell against the county whose staff he will join later in the season. The team’s captain is Michael Atherton and the coach Graham Saville of Essex who has as good a knowledge as anyone of the realities of cricket at school and university level. I trust that Ted Dexter will be having some discussions with him about how the current haphazard ‘system’ of youthful cricket can be improved. I should be surprised if Saville does not feel, as I do, that in Atherton England have a ready-made captain for the long-term future. I mean long-term in both senses: he is not ready yet but, if all goes well, one would like to see him getting the job at the age of about 25 and keeping it for at least seven years.

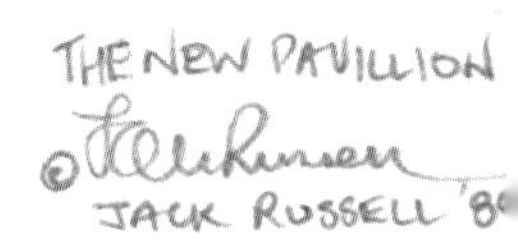

Saturday, April 29th

I travelled to Taunton through a good deal of rain this morning, not too hopeful of seeing any cricket when I got there, but agreeably surprised when I did. En route I listened to the broadcast on Radio Four of the Memorial Service in Liverpool Cathedral for the 95 spectators who had been crushed to death in the overcrowded stand at Hillsborough a fortnight before. The Bishop, David Sheppard, led an imaginative and moving service with his customary excellence. His sister, Mary, lives in our village at Rudgwick and worships with us at the parish church. She is justly proud of her brother's eminence and although their father died young, cricket was always an important part of their lives at the neighbouring village of Slinfold.

At Taunton play began in cold weather before a sparse crowd at 12.15 and although Somerset started the day in a comanding position, Glamorgan had the better of the rest of the day. Stephen Barwick bowled unchanged from the new Pavilion end and deservedly took seven wickets against batting which was meek and unenterprising when it came to taking

advantage of the plentiful supply of bad balls bowled at the other end. The culprits, I'm afraid, were the young spinners, North and Cann, though the latter (bowling mainly because Ontong is still recovering from a knee injury suffered last season in a motorway crash) looks a good, enthusiastic little cricketer.

Barwick bowled mainly off-cutters off his usual medium-pacer's run-up. He uses his height well and is putting into effect the lessons taught him by Don Shepherd, whose off-breaks are talked about with some reverence in Welsh cricketing circles. The best batting of the day came from Jimmy Cook, the schoolmaster from Johannesburg, who has already impressed everyone at Taunton as both batsman and man, and from the two best Glamorgan batsmen, Hugh Morris and Matthew Maynard. I have never seen Hugh Morris play better. He was solid and correct but swift to put away the bad ball. I have often sung the praises of his namesake, John, the talented but inconsistent Derbyshire batsman, but I think, in time we may hear more about Hugh. Indeed if Atherton were not to develop as everyone hopes he will, another Welsh captain of England is not beyond possibility.

Maynard, who certainly doesn't lack confidence and whom I find a most engaging character, has had a dreadful start the season after spending the winter in Perth (West Australia, not West Scotland!). He hit three or four boundaries of marvellous pedigree in pale evening sunshine. I am sure he will be making a big score or two before long. He is particularly good through the covers off the back foot but he does tend to give himself room in that area and I don't like the thought of his going to the West Indies early next year. It might nip a ripening talent in the bud.

The small crowd meant little atmosphere and it was not easy trying to 'sell' the match to sports producers far more interested in the promotion and relegation battles of the eternal football season.

At lunchtime I chatted to Alan Gibson, who learned the art of commentary in an era when county cricket was much more generously covered by the BBC. He was tucked snugly in the bar all day, watching the cricket through a window, cheerful and articulate still despite an illness which prevents his walking other than with the aid of a frame.

MAY

Monday, May 1st

Instead of going to see the finish of the Taunton game (which Glamorgan saved, with some honour) I was sent nearer home, to Hove, it being deemed that there was more cricket left in the match. Alas it was typical Bank Holiday weather by the sea. A mist hovered over the Downs all day and it frequently drizzled hard enough to stop play. The umpires did very well, I thought, to get in as much play as they did. Kent were in a hole at the start of the day but Mark Benson set himself to bat with total single-mindedness through the day and in the afternoon there was an innings of immense promise by Trevor Ward. He turned bouncers into long-hops, pulling four of them (two from the sometimes thoughtless Babington) into the seedy old Pavilion.

Tuesday, May 2nd

I went to Ealing Cricket Club today to see the Australians practising. The summer has arrived and it was a most beautiful morning. But all I could find when I arrived was the young groundsman, Peter Craig, rolling a most appealing looking square. The Aussies had rung him the night before to say they were not going to pitch up! Still, 'all places that the eye of heaven meets are, to a wise man, ports and happy havens.' I have a theory that no day, no experience in life is ever wasted. Instead of seeing the Australians I saw a ground I had

THE COLLEGE GRO
© JACK RUSSE

heard a lot about but never played at (Ealing have long been one of the best clubs in Middlesex) and I met a groundsman who was so friendly, keen and helpful that I would back him to be looking after a county or Test ground before long. He comes from Lancashire and did his apprenticeship at Old Trafford.

Thursday, May 4th

Whilst Jack Russell's Gloucestershire were embarking on a high scoring draw against Glamorgan at Cardiff – better than last year when their match at Swansea was abandoned without a ball being bowled – I was leading MCC into a friendly battle against my old school Marlborough on 'the XI', always a lovely place to play. I had a strong batting side and Neil Hames, the Buckinghamshire left-hander, who is trying to qualify as a playing member, did his stuff with a fine 70 odd, but our bowling, even with an ex-England player in Richard Hutton, was treated strictly on its dubious merits, our fielding was less than skittish and the School recorded a famous victory in the final over. Their talented all-rounder Ed Longfield hit a marvellously carefree and uninhibited maiden 100. I shall propose him for MCC membership at once!

Sunday, May 7th

Despite a chilly wind, this was a day, like the last three or four have been, of flawless sunshine. The West Sussex countryside was quite breathtakingly beautiful, almost all the trees now fully out but still in their earliest lime green compared with the darker verdancy of the evergreens and the lusher, meadow green of the rolling Downs; all this under a sky of purest blue which showed not a shadow of a cloud all day. Somehow on such days the eyes ignore the low, cheap factory buildings which are sprouting up around Sussex as they are everywhere else and will be seen in time as the architectural blight of the Eighties. Instead I noticed only the harmonious timber-framed and brick and flint cottages which typify this special part of England. What is more, although everyone else seemed to get stuck in a traffic jam as a crowd of well over 10,000 inched towards Arundel – and a few more thousands made their way along the same road to the Coast – I was lucky. I have never been a great navigator but managed for once to take a successful back route both ways, so there was time to get the lawn mowed in two sessions, soon after dawn and just before dusk.

It was one of those entirely satisfactory days in that the match itself was worth watching and the producer of *Sunday Sport* was interested enough in the event to give plenty of airtime to me and my ABC colleague, Neville Oliver from Tasmania, a live-wire character squarely built with red hair and a red face rather like David Bairstow. I worked with him in Australia last time and although I was sorry that Jim Maxwell did not get the job in succession to Alan McGilvray, because I think he knows his cricket even more fully than Neville, the latter is an excellent all round broadcaster who will fit in very well, I'm sure, with *Test Match Special*.

The Duchess of Norfolk's ground can never have looked more lovely, and all the 'workers' of Arundel cricket, Ronnie Ford, Debbie Osborne, Colin Cowdrey, John Barclay, etc., were smiling all day. So were all the sunbathing spectators. The Australians made a little matter of 314 for 6 in their 50 overs (they made over 300 in their other limited-over warm-up game at West Bromwich last week) with David Boon, the imperious Tom Moody, Allan Border and Steve Waugh all hitting the ball with impressive ease. The Duchess's side comprised mainly Leicestershire players and succumbed meekly. Merv Hughes bowled especially well.

Wednesday, May 10th

I went to see my younger son, Robin, playing for his prep school, Cranleigh, against Woodcote House at Bagshot today. In his first two matches he had scored 53 and 69 and taken 5 for 21 and 8 for 10. He is tall for his age, 13 $^1/_2$, and has always been mad keen on the game – even as a baby the best way to calm him down when he was unhappy about something was to get a ball out. He has played with success in a useful Sussex Under 13 side; and, after a modest season with the bat for his school last season, he owed them some runs in his third year in the side and as captain. He has certainly not let himself down. By the time I had found the school today he had taken six more wickets and he added a seventh as I arrived, causing me to shatter my wing mirror against the Cranleigh School bus (shades of Colin Cowdrey who was so excited when he heard on the radio that his son Christopher got his first Test wicket that he drove the wrong way down a one-way street!).

Relieved to find that I had inflicted damage only to my own car, I emerged a little shamefaced to see the Woodcote number eleven avert the hat-trick. One wicketless over later the captain took himself off! He learned a hard lesson thereby because from 22 for nine the opposition took their score to 92 before the partnership was broken by a run-out. The two home heroes played very well on a sloping, fast-scoring ground but the Cranleigh boys fielded well too, even if their skipper failed to encourage them, being too pre-occupied, when he came back on, with his sudden loss of wicket-taking magic.

All ended well, anyway. Surviving a stumping chance against a very promising off-spinner also destined for Radley, by the name of Ross-Brown, M-J junior scored 53 while his younger team-mates picked up enough to earn a third successive victory. There is nothing worse than a boastful father and I shall be perfectly happy if my two sons become good club cricketers but it is immensely enjoyable, as well as very tense, to watch one's sons in action having tried to put them on the right lines in the garden. A 'phone call to Radley elicited the fact that James had made 50 for the Radley Colts against Cheltenham on Saturday so both of them are at present having the necessary fortune and making the most of their ability. I hope they will do likewise in their exams in a month's time!

Saturday, May 13th

Another triumph for young cricketers today. For the first time the Combined Universities, having achieved a marvellous win in mid-week over Worcestershire and having today scored enough runs at a fast enough rate against Gloucestershire, have qualified for the quarter-finals of the Benson and Hedges. This is the first time they have ever achieved this, the first, indeed, that they have ever seriously threatened to do so. There has been absolutely no fluke about it. It won't happen but what a thrill if they were to get to the final at Lord's!

I was at New Road, Worcester today to see an extraordinary day's play between the Champion county and the Australian touring team. When a shower brought an early end to the play, 24 wickets had fallen, ten of them to Philip Newport who swung the ball all day as well as using a quickish pitch of unreliable bounce to seam it around waspishly. Radford, Alderman, Lawson and Waugh also enjoyed bowling on it. Despite accomplished innings by Curtis and

Botham (46 and 39) Worcestershire could only achieve a lead of 43 and even Hick, dropped once in a struggling innings of 13, found the varying height at which the ball pitched too difficult to overcome.

The Worcester square looks much, much better than it did toward the second half of last season when the dedicated groundsman, Roy McLaren, had to prepare pitches for 29 out of 31 days in August on a square which only has room for 11 pitches. His problem is not the 'holes' into which the *Sunday Times* correspondent reported he had sunk his car keys but the mixture of fine and coarse grasses, something not only Worcester is suffering from. There is also the question of the balls being used by an increasing number of counties this season. The Reader ball has a more prominent seam than its rival, the Twort, and although it maintains its shape better it certainly helps the seamers.

Monday, May 15th

I awoke at half past six at the pleasant Fownes Hotel on a gentle, sunny morning and walked across to Worcester Cathedral for the eight o'clock Communion Service.

Afterwards I strolled for a while in the Cathedral precincts: swans glided on the Severn below and the Malvern Hills, beloved of Edward Elgar, were blue in the distance. The only sound was of birds singing. How many souls have found solace from this foretaste of heaven since the great red sandstones of the Cathedral were heaved into place to the grand design of a mediaeval architect nine centuries ago?

There was a good-sized crowd again at New Road the other side of the river and they had a tense, absorbing day's cricket to watch. At first Border and Waugh kept Newport and Radford at bay, Waugh needing a bit more luck than his captain, who was at his grittiest and most skilful. But Waugh was lbw to Botham for a 63 containing 11 fours and Border bowled by a ball of full length from Newport for 48 before Radford polished the innings off for 205. Radford's match figures were 7 for 90, Newport's a selectors' eye-catching 11 for 128, the best by a Worcester bowler against the Australians since 1902.

Worcestershire began batting in mid-afternoon and at seven o'clock edged home by three wickets for their first win against an Australian touring team, despite classy bowling from Alderman and Lawson. Hick, 43, and Botham, 42, were chiefly responsible. The pitch may not have been much fun to bat on but it made it a wonderful game to watch. Worcestershire get a share of the £25,000 kitty available for county games against the tourists.

Thursday, May 18th

I played for Horsham's convivial Thursday side today. The fixtures are almost all at home but today's was an exception, played away at Steyning for the Tom Crowe trophy which is competed for twice a season somewhat less earnestly than the Ashes or even the Sussex League. Tom was a stalwart bowler for the Thursday side and these days always scores while his wife helps with the teas. On such marvellous devotees of the game our clubs have always relied.

We usually have some pretty good cricketers playing on Thursdays and went through last season undefeated although, as I say, no-one would have lost any sleep had we been beaten. We did, however, have a severe embarrassment last year in this same fixture when only six men arrived to represent the club, amongst them Richard de Groen, who may well go on to play Test cricket for New Zealand. He is tall, strong and quite quick; it was as well he wasn't on parade today because something awful has happened to Steyning's square.

It was a most wonderful May day, sunny and heavily warm, the trees pregnant with verdant growth and everywhere Maythorn making creamy white splashes only slightly less vivid than the cow parsley (some prefer parsnip) now rising high on all grass verges. Steyning's ground, moreover, is perfectly set in the lea of the South Downs with old white-painted, mellow roofed houses along one side and a smart white pavilion whose facilities would hardly shame a county side. But a club is in peril if its pitches are bad and we were amazed when we sauntered out to field at half past two to find a strip comprised of large clumps of dead straw coloured grass – it looked like couch grass – interspersed with crumbling grey earth.

In practice the ball kept low frequently, turned a long way very slowly and occasionally popped gently, but the members, who look after the square themselves, though the ground is council-owned, have a massive job ahead of them. Apparently they neglected the square last autumn and this spring in the hope that the Council would spend some money on new equipment, but they may be the sufferers from their own strategy. At any rate they made 140 all out against a moderate Horsham attack, none too well supported in the field. Our Barbados born all-rounder Winston Weekes was absent ill, thus reducing us to nine men since this week's captain, Richard Bond, a schoolmaster at Christ's Hospital, had spent a fortune on 'phone calls and still started one short.

I played only on condition that I left at six o'clock, having contracted to speak at a dinner near Melksham, but the shambles (which also included the captain suffering a dislocated finger as he took a catch at mid-off and a Steyning fielder sustaining a sickening blow in the jaw standing at silly mid-off) looked like having a happy ending when I left. My early departure (a subtle ploy) meant that I had to open and I managed about 30 of an opening stand of 52 with a New Zealander with first-class experience, Craig Ashton, before retiring, with only a few bruises on fingers and wrists, for a quick shower and a hasty drive towards the setting sun. I shall find out in a fortnight if we managed to get the runs.

I am playing for Albury in the Three Counties League on Saturday, to keep in touch with that fine little club in the village where my wife and I lived when we were first married, but after that, alas, my own cricket will become even more irregular. Once or twice in recent years I have considered giving up altogether but I really feel I can commentate and report the game better when I have had recent experience of playing, at whatever level. It is easy, otherwise, to forget how difficult a game it can be, and also how uplifting when you have a good day, especially when the weather is as lovely as it was today.

Incidentally another of Horsham's occasional colonial cousins, Tim May, took three for 38 for the Australians at Taunton today and his side look like beating Somerset.

Saturday, May 20th

It being Cup Final day (Liverpool beat Everton after extra time) I was free to play for Albury against Haslemere in the Three Counties League. The Haslemere ground is prettily situated and for a council owned ground is well cared for, though not as well as Albury's which benefits from the entirely voluntary labour of Rowland Woods and Vic Rollands. It was another sweltering day and when Haslemere, whom Albury had beaten three times out of three in different competitions last year, put us in, we felt it was because they thought that they might be set a target and have a good chance of getting the runs.

In the event the target we set them was 66 to win! The ball swung around all over the place and one of their opening bowlers took six for 30 with genuinely late inswingers at a lively pace. Having come in at nought for three I hung around for six or seven overs then sliced a drive to gully, a terrible waste of a lovely day for batting.

When he came in to bat with Haslemere 59 for five and not yet absolutely certain to win – thanks to fine swing bowling in turn by Jeff Austin – the young Haslemere number seven petulantly and unexpectedly threw his bat down when Albury's captain made a perfectly reasonable if slightly belated change of field as our young fast bowler, Mike Gore, was about to run in. Having been advised that he could go home to his mother if he preferred, the batsman carved the first ball over cover for four, missed a hook at a sharp bouncer from Gore next ball, and was then bowled having a very wild swing at the next. Thereupon he spreadeagled the stumps even further with his bat and, on being admonished by all the close fielders, came close to assaulting the captain, a born fighter himself, Dr Martin Smith, who survived only because, it seemed, the dismissed batsman could not decide whether to strangle him or hit him over the head with his avenging bat.

All this would rightly have been condemned had it happened (*sans* bat) at Wembley, let alone Haslemere Recreation Ground. It all seemed very irrational to me, especially as Haslemere had had a very good day (they duly got the last three runs) but I was reminded that a few seasons ago Albury, having fielded throughout a Haslemere innings in the rain in another league match had got to the point of victory in reply, whereupon the Haslemere umpire had uprooted the stumps and said that he had no intention of remaining out in the rain any longer! In other words the fixture has a 'history'.

It was a reminder that amateur sportsmen can behave every bit as badly as professionals and often take themselves far, far too seriously. It also raised the question in my mind, once again, of what cricket in the South has lost or gained from the fact that these days club matches are played for points. This sort of incident *must* be more likely to happen in league cricket than it was in the old days of 'friendlies' but honest players of old will agree that there have always been intense rivalries between certain clubs and characters who get over excited or rub their opponents up the wrong way.

Wednesday, May 24th

I left home at 9.30 after mowing the smaller lawn and got to Manchester at two, just as thunder and lightning was interrupting England's net practice.

Thanks to the unseasonal weather, the Australians will go into the three one-day internationals which start at Old Trafford tomorrow much better prepared than most recent touring teams. Their one serious injury today, to Dean Jones's jaw, is now mended, the main bowlers are in form, notably the key fast men Rackemann, Lawson and Alderman and all the batsmen except Veletta have some good scores and several hours at the crease behind them. The impression is of a confident, hard-working, efficient side ready for bigger challenges.

These One-Day Internationals can be magnificent occasions in themselves but large red herrings when it comes to judging the prospects of a Test series. For this reason I would much prefer to see them played at the end of the season when the holiday mood is abroad. What a pleasant consolation it would have been last season, for instance, had England won all three games *after* being trounced in the Test series. Had you forgotten that the result of the three matches played this time last year was, indeed, England three, West Indies nil? M'lud may look incredulous, but if I may be so bold as to suggest that he should check the facts?

This, of course, puts these games into their proper place: which is not to say that they will not be taken very seriously by the players and by the spectators who have bought all available tickets for all three games at Manchester tomorrow, Trent Bridge on Thursday and Lord's on Monday. Rightly or wrongly these matches will be seen to portend much of significance for the Tests ahead. But we must hope that the new England selection committee of three – Ted Dexter, Chairman; Micky Stewart, Manager; and David Gower, Captain – will not make the mistake of their predecessors in setting too much store by performances in matches which put a premium

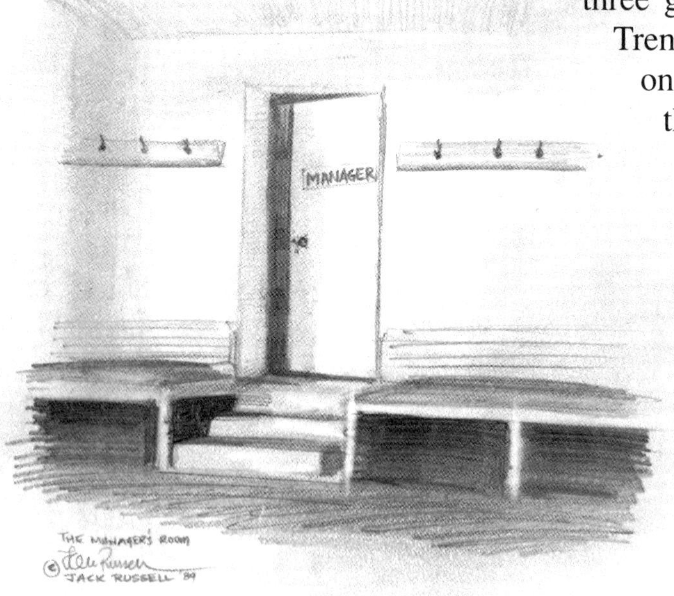

on defensive bowling and enterprising batting; especially the former.

Already there are worrying signs. It was hardly logical, for instance, for Dexter to mention Ian Botham's brilliant slip catching this season as a reason for his selection for games in which after a few overs there may well be no slip fielders at all. It might have been wiser to keep Botham for later appearances in the Tests, giving him two more matches for Worcestershire in the hope of his producing a performance or two to convince everyone that he deserves to be chosen on present performance as well as past reputation.

From what I have seen of Botham's bowling this season he would not be likely to pick up more than, say, 12 wickets if he were to play for England through the entire Test series. In other words he would be a useful fourth seamer but not any more a front-line bowler. This means in most circumstances that four specialist bowlers would need to play which in turn means Botham batting at six and no place for one of the three specialist batsmen, Gatting, Lamb and Robin Smith, all in prime form at present.

Whatever happens in the next week one would expect that for Headingley Chris Broad will be preferred to Kim Barnett, Jack Russell to Steve Rhodes, and Phil Newport to Philip De Freitas. One cannot argue, however, with the choice of one day specialists for one-day matches. De Freitas has started the season with great success and has been very effective for England in one-day cricket; Barnett is a versatile batsman with an ideal temperament; and Rhodes may well develop into England's first really Test class wicket-keeper/batsman since Alan Knott. He would have to keep very well indeed, however, to be preferred to Russell for the Tests.

Form in limited-overs cricket is not really relevant but Australia will take added comfort from the fact that they have beaten England on the last two occasions they have played under limited-overs rules: at Melbourne in the Bi-Centenary game and in the World Cup Final at Calcutta. For all that, England are more likely to take the Texaco trophy and the lion's share of the total prize money of £141,300.

Thursday, May 25th

I got to the ground at eight for my live 'piece' on the *Today* programme. The ground staff were hard at work on the main ground, and the umpires John Holder and Nigel Plews were busy chatting with Peter Marron.

Brian Johnston, myself and Neville Oliver were the commentators, with Fred Trueman and Trevor Bailey as summarisers, Peter Baxter as producer, and Bill Frindall as scorer. It was fun to be back in action even if the game we had to describe was rather one-sided because of the flying start given to England by Gooch and Gower, with the contrastingly poor start made by Australia against De Freitas and Foster. From 17 for three they never looked like getting anywhere near England's eventually only fair total of 231 for nine.

Gower played some brilliant strokes in the first few overs and off only 33 balls hit five of only 13 fours in the innings plus a sumptuous hook off Lawson, who tended to give too much width to Gower's willowy swing of the bat. But wickets fell unexpectedly: Gower half changed his mind about fiddling at a ball from Rackeman who, along with Alderman, bowled well; Gooch played a soft little paddle sweep in the last over before lunch and got a top edge; and Smith, when going like a cruise ship at full steam, popped a catch back to the bowler. But for these three accidents England would have scored nearer 280. As it was they were grateful for some untidyness in the field as De Freitas and Emburey scrambled expertly in the last few overs.

The decisive moment in the Australian innings was the demonic ball from Foster which cut back inside Border's defences from a long way outside off-stump. Both Newport (for Worcestershire) and Foster have discovered that Border has no liking at all for sharp inswing. Since Boon, so full of early-tour runs, had already played a confident drive at a good length ball from the lively De Freitas and lost his off-stump, and Jones, in only his second innings since fracturing a bone in his face when mis-hooking Pigott at Hove, had been caught down the leg-side, the gifted, combative Waugh was left with too much to do. Marsh appeared

'THE BELL, OLD TRAFFORD'
© JACK RUSSELL '89

to settle for batting practice and the game faded to a predictably low-key finish.

Emburey bowled better than he has for a long time. The man of the match adjudicator, Clive Lloyd, chose De Freitas ahead of two more obvious candidates, Gower and Foster. These 'Lancastrians' have to stick together!

Friday, May 26th

I played golf this morning at the elegant Mere Course with John Thicknesse, Tony Lewis, Jack Bannister and Mike Selvey. Lewis took the stapleford money and Thicknesse took mine off me as he usually does, but it was such a lovely morning that, even spraying balls everywhere, I greatly enjoyed it.

Since the BBC were on strike there was no cause for me to rush to Trent Bridge and I managed to take well over four hours meandering across the edge of the Peak District towards Southwell, where I nearly always stay for matches at Nottingham. The weather remained lovely and I stopped for half a pint and a read of the papers near Leek, not one of Britain's better known beauty spots but beautiful for all that.

I dined at the Saracens Head, after doing some work, with Baxter and Brough Scott, the *Sunday Times* columnist who was up to do a piece on Botham's return. He is a first-class writer, especially, of course, on his own sport of horse-racing.

Saturday, May 27th

Another sunny morning. I had escaped the really early start but was at Trent Bridge in time for a chat with Cliff Morgan on Radio Four just after nine. Ron Alsopp was his usual cheery self when I inspected his pitch before going up to our perfectly situated commentary box, though I have come to take what Ron says about the preparation of his pitches with a slight pinch of salt. He would have preferred a little rain to help but although a thunderstorm earlier in week had flooded the outfield, making it very slow, the pitch itself had not been touched. It must, however, have been watered because it was even slower than the one at Old Trafford and run scoring was hard labour.

Alderman and Rackemann again allowed the three Gs less liberty than Lawson but this time Australia had rightly selected a fifth 'serious' bowler and May did well after lunch to beat Gatting on the outside of an offside push and then to beat Smith in the air. Smith certainly *used* to be a relatively poor player of spin: that cancelled tour of India could have given him valuable experience.

It was not May's fault that England, badly behind their tactical rate of scoring, were allowed to pick up runs far too easily in a third wicket stand of 62 between Lamb and Gatting. Border still seems to captain by a stereotyped rule book, instead of fitting his tactics to events and conditions. May was given only four men to save the singles and, of course, they didn't because the England pair thankfully and comfortably worked him into the gaps. Botham entered at 123 for four with enough overs,14, to stake his claim to a Test place, but after making eight comfortable runs off 15 balls he was brilliantly thrown out by Border from mid-wicket.

It was now, in the last 12 overs, that Lamb, effectively and sensibly partnered by Pringle, moved out of his sports car into a Formula One. The timing of his attacking shots took the breath away. The best punchers in boxing, they say, deliver knockout blows from close in, compressing their force into a short, lethal swing of the fist. Lamb is rather the same: his bat meets the ball with a late, staccato punch. It was a surprise to see after he had reached his 100 off the last ball of the innings, his last 50 coming off 34 balls, that he had hit only nine fours. Each one of them was memorable.

Australia, perhaps encouraged by Lamb's freedom, were never so inhibited as England had been earlier, although the pitch and the outfield had quickened perceptibly under the unyielding sun. Boon and Waugh gave a positive lead and Border and Waugh followed up with confident, commanding batting. Yet Australia found funny ways of getting out. Of the two run-outs the saddest for them was that of Waugh, trying a second run to Gooch after Healy had slipped and twisted his knee.

Healy remained to the last over, when seven were needed. He briefly employed Jones as a runner, until, forgetting himself, he ran two runs even faster than Jones. Gower politely suggested that if he could run that fast he ought to run his own runs. In the end he managed a bye off the final ball, which Rackemann missed, to secure a tie. England, however, were deemed to be winners of the Texaco trophy because they had lost fewer wickets. They were lucky to get away with it because they bowled seven wides in the innings, four of them in the later stages. On the other hand, apart from a bad miss at slip by, of all people, Botham, they fielded better than Australia.

Monday, May 29th

The drive to London was painless for once and 25,000 at Lord's had joyful entertainment. Only in the first few overs was batting anything other than straightforward and Gower, having won the toss for the third time, was soon matching Gooch stroke for stroke in an opening partnership of 123. A shirt-sleeved crowd of 24,000 contained a good many youngsters on a half-term treat and they can only have found the occasion inspiring. They saw some beautifully controlled swing and seam bowling by Alderman but otherwise it was a day when bowlers were like the attendants of models at a dress show: merely on hand to help the batsmen show off their finery. (As a matter of fact one 19-year-old decided that she could best show off *without* any clothes and ran diagonally across the ground towards the Warner Stand in the fairest streak seen at Lord's before the end of May.) Such adornment was unnecessary.

Gooch stayed, after Gower had been acrobatically caught by the reserve wicket-keeper, to play the major innings, his batting apparently unsubtle to the untrained eye but in fact notable for his ability not just to drive the ball immensely hard, always along the ground, but also to place it by careful adjustment of the feet and angling of the blade. Gatting and Smith lent busy support, the former being the second Englishman in three days to fall to the accuracy of Border's close-range throwing, but neither was as effective as Botham who, really letting himself go for the first time this season, crashed three fours and a straight six in the course of scoring 25 off 11 balls.

Australia had to play really well to score the runs – 279 at five runs an over – but score them they did, with three balls to spare. Boon got them away to a rapid start and Marsh stayed to anchor the innings expertly without ever getting bogged down. He is a tremendous trier.

Jones had played himself in carefully, ready for an assault after tea, but he then chipped Emburey to Gower at mid-on. The next ball, Border's first, was driven for four and the skipper proceeded to 50 off 40 balls. He played brilliantly and Waugh followed him with unruffled confidence, virtually settling the issue with successive sixes, cleanly struck off Foster into the Tavern.

Australia will now know they can beat England. In theory their problems will come in the field. They have one or two slow coaches and their bowlers will need some help from the pitches if they are going to bowl England out twice in the Tests. Not that England's are much better, but they have Newport plus, perhaps, Jarvis and Fraser and soon, touch wood, Dilley, in reserve.

I got home at 9.30 with my sons James and Robin, having left home at 8.00. A long, exciting day.

Wednesday, May 31st

I left home very early for Chelmsford to report and commentate on the Benson and Hedges quarter-final tie between Essex and Lancashire. It is necessary to arrive early on these occaions if you want to get your car into the ground, but there is seldom the problem with hostile gatemen at Chelmsford that there is at so many grounds. Essex is the model of how a county club should be run. They have profited from making success on the field their first priority, looking after all the members of their staff whether they be Test stars or youngsters carefully selected after progression from junior teams. The locally produced talent is augmented by a hand-picked player from overseas and one or two disillusioned exiles from

The view from The Tavern at Bristol

other clubs like John Childs and Geoff Miller.

The business side of the club positively hums, too. The Chief Executive, Peter Edwards, a bright chap in all senses who, like all county secretaries, works extremely hard, is allowed to get on with his job. Everyone seems to know and like him, from occasional stewards to visiting journalists. The small committee, with Doug Insole in urbane, self-effacing command, exists to help the club not the other way round. Profits made from energetic selling to local businesses have been ploughed back into facilities on the compact little ground, which get better every year.

Compact is the word for our BBC commentary box, too. Our scorer for the day, Peter Byrne, is built on generous lines and to have him together with Colin Milburn in the little wooden hut would mean no room for a commentator. Fortunately my colleagues today were Derek Underwood, conscientious as ever, and Ralph Dellor, both slim men, so we squeezed in three at a time and shared coverage with the three other ties in the first ever all-day transmission of the quarter finals. Match of the day (I knew it would be, but Henry Blofeld had got to Peter Baxter first!) was the one at Taunton between Somerset and the Combined Universities. The undergraduates very nearly beat the county, Nasser Hussain playing a brilliant innings and Michael Atherton taking four wickets with his leg-breaks but the coolness of a former Cambridge man, Peter Roebuck, saved Somerset at the pulsating climax of the match.

Our game was never predictable, Essex eventually managing to reach Lancashire's considerable target despite a rare failure by Gooch. They were indebted to skilfully unorthodox batting by Brian 'Lager' Hardie and a more classical innings of high class by Steve Waugh's twin brother, Mark.

At Bristol Gloucestershire lost to Nottinghamshire much more narrowly than had seemed likely for much of the day, the illustrator of this book making 57 to take Gloucestershire to the last over needing only 9. Unfortunately Jack holed out to the second ball and Notts squeezed home by five runs, thankful to Chris Broad for a solid hundred to add to the two centuries he got in the Championship against Glamorgan last weekend. That will surely have made sure of his return to Test cricket and his original county of Gloucestershire could do with his batting this season. So far the switch of captaincy from Graveney to Athey does not seem to have done the trick.

The fourth of today's ties was won by Kent, a most unexpected and therefore admirable win at Northampton where the home team seemed sure to win when restricting Kent to a score of only just over 200. Curtley Ambrose, by whom Northants had set much store this season, was their most expensive bowler. Maybe in the end it will prove a blessing for Northamptonshire not to get to another Lord's final and, perhaps, lose again. They ought, in my view, to win the Championship and it will do them no harm if they concentrate their main energies on doing so.

I got home from Chelmsford at about 11 o'clock. They are long days, these big one-day occasions. My long suffering wife had an even longer one, however, driving James all the way to Colchester to play for Sussex Under-16s against Essex (they won and he scored 11 not out) and then taking him all the way back to Radley. Poor Judy, having long since given up watching me play cricket, now spends much of her time ferrying her two sons about to matches, going to watch them as a loyal mother and baking cakes for cricket teas.

JUNE

Thursday, June 1st

I batted on a beautiful pitch today, at Horsham, where I went in at number four at 85 for two against Cantonians, a side of decent Essex club cricketers from clubs like Brentwood, Southend and North Middlesex, whose off-spinner, John Beale, bowled particularly accurately. Yet when I joined Winston Weekes, our Bajan Wandering Star had already scored about 70 and just over two hours later we declared at 305 for two. Winston made 178 not out, I managed 72 not out without playing many really satisfying strokes. It was one of those bone-hard pitches on which you find it hard to make a mark with your bat when you take guard and Winston, smiling most of the time and laughing the rest, drove and cut the ball to all parts of the scenic ground on a grey, cool afternoon. Although Cantonians were given an equal time to bat they were never in touch with the necessary rate. It won't happen again so I might as well boast and record my figures of three for 16! We dismissed eight of them, but too late to wheedle out the last two. 'Jeg' the Groundsman and his roller were the real heroes.

Wednesday, June 7th

Having been at full stretch recently, I had not got the main lawn mown and had to mow it wet this morning at 7.30 before leaving at nine for Leeds. Fortunately I had a clear run up the M1 despite travelling through frequent showers and the weather at Headingley was not too bad. Deloittes were giving a party to publicise their form ratings of current players. This was the brainchild of Ted Dexter whose committee had chosen the following original 12 for the first Cornhill Test: Broad, Gooch, Gatting, Gower, Lamb, Botham, Pringle, Emburey, Russell, De Freitas, Newport, and Foster.

Since this combination was announced on Saturday morning – I own to criticising the choices of Botham, De Freitas and Emburey, in whose places I would have had Smith, Jarvis or Fraser and Medlycott or Childs – Gatting has become a doubtful starter because of a fracture to his left thumb whilst taking a brilliant slip catch on Sunday, and Botham has been ruled out after top-edging a hook against Steve Barwick at Worcester and sustaining a depressed fracture of the right cheek bone. This was rotten luck for both men, considering their unhappy time in 1988 for differing reasons. Botham, especially, had worked very hard to get fit and there was great expectation in many places about his return to the scene of his greatest triumph.

Smith, who should never have been left out in the form he was in, replaced Botham, and Barnett was called up as reserve for Gatting, who had a longish net this afternoon at about the time that Nashwan was running away with the Derby. I watched the race with Joe Lister, the courteous Yorkshire secretary, in his office. He had backed the winner at 16 to 1. I had backed a horse called Observation Post on the recommendation of Barry Hills at Manton in December. Alas, it never got to the Starting Post, let alone the Observation Post – certainly not to the Winning Post!

I am no better at predicting pitches than I am winners of horse races but the Test strip produced with loving care by Keith Boyce in the middle of his unnaturally green square (which looks like a bowling green or the Centre Court at Wimbledon before tennis

begins) has fewer cracks than usual and produced a great many runs when Yorkshire played Middlesex last year on it. It was dug up in 1986 by Boyce who told me this afternoon that he had found dreadful, crumbling soil 18 inches down. The replacement soil is settling down now, he feels, and should soon form the base of a really good wicket. Ladbroke's make a draw the favourite in view of the pitch and the weather and they had made Nashwan favourite too, so who will argue?

Thursday, June 8th

On a cold, grey day Australia were put into bat by David Gower and scored 207 for three, Mark Taylor batting all day for 96 not out in his first Test innings against England. In the interview I did with him yesterday Gower said, 'I would be loath to go into this game without a spinner.' It is already obvious that he should not have allowed his advisers to change his mind for him. England should have batted and Emburey, having been selected in thc 12, should have played to give variety to the attack. As it was De Freitas, Foster, Newport and Pringle got little assistance from a pitch which Fred Trueman correctly predicted on Radio Three would be 'slow and low'. The ball did far less than it usually does at Headingley and Border played an exciting, aggressive innings of 66 with nine fours to complement Taylor's solid, doughty effort.

It was pleasant, as always, to return this evening through gorgeous 'Herriot Country' to the Devonshire Arms just near Bolton Abbey in Wharfedale. Bolton Abbey's cricket ground is tucked in between the grey stone of the hotel and two grey-stone arches of the road bridge over the River Wharfe. Beyond, the eye travels across lush green fields to the bare-topped Moor. The rich pasture is shared by sheep and cattle and the scent of mingled grass and sheep droppings fills the nostrils. A mile away, along a foot-path which runs parallel to the river, is the noble ruin of the Augustinian Priory of Bolton Abbey.

A curious thing happened soon after I got back. Some village cricketers, one or two in white, most still in their working clothes, pegged out a net and began to practise. The instant they started a herd of bullocks in the next field went galumphing up to the wooden post and rail fence for all the world as if to watch the first ball of a Test Match. They peered over while a few balls were bowled, then, as if unimpressed, returned to their grazing.

I went for a short walk and spotted dippers, mallard, curlew, pied wagtails, sand-martins and black-headed gulls. Last year I also saw an otter.

I had a good meal in the convivial company of Peter Baxter, John Thicknesse and Brian and Audrey Scovell. Ted Dexter is joining us tomorrow and will perhaps have some explaining to do!

Friday, June 9th

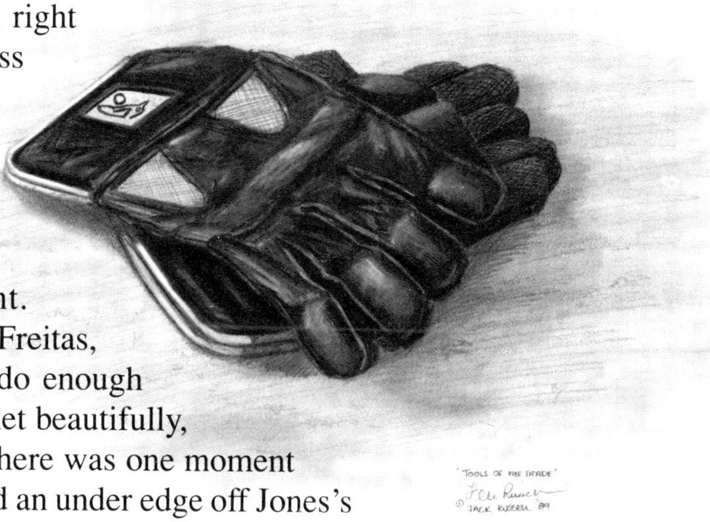

Australia rubbed salt in the wound today and Steve Waugh made a brilliant first Test hundred off only 124 balls. His square-cutting and cleanly stroked clips off his legs were classical, as indeed was his whole innings. He was always sideways on, quick to pick up the length and to get right forward or right back and ruthless with every bad ball he received. Although Foster bowled very well today, and Newport much better, England's bowling generally was stereotyped and inconsistent. Pringle was not at his best and De Freitas, hard as he tried, just does not do enough with the ball. Russell kept wicket beautifully, despite frequent low bounce. There was one moment when he seemed to have dropped an under edge off Jones's bat, but apparently it came from the pad. That is what Jones said, anyway, and Umpire John Holder told Jack that he would not have given it out.

Taylor duly got his hundred and celebrated with a succession of merry cover-drives, and Jones ran like a hare for both Taylor and Waugh as well as playing some fine shots himself. He was dropped once by Barnett, otherwise England's best fielder. Although Healy missed the pleasure boat, Mervyn Hughes emphatically did not: 63 not out!

Saturday, June 10th

Another good day's cricket and so different from all recent Headingley Tests. Australia declared after 24 minutes at 601 for seven, Waugh 177 not out. Hughes was out for 71 to the third successive bouncer bowled at him by Foster. Lawson got the same treatment but survived it until Border let him loose with the new ball.

Alderman, getting close to the stumps and nipping the ball either way, tested Gooch before having him lbw, but Broad played with reassuring calm and comfort until Hughes completely and triumphantly deceived him with a slow leg-break.

Happily, on a fine, sunny afternoon and with the ground almost full, Lamb and Barnett counter-attacked splendidly. The truth was that batting was a very pleasant business with the pitch now playing very easily, the outfield quick and relatively small and the supply of bad balls plentiful enough if not so liberally supplied as they had been by England. Barnett and Lamb put on 114 in 28 overs, Barnett light as a dancer on his feet and quick of eye too, Lamb carrying on as he had batted for England a fortnight before and for Northants more recently. The dry summer is suiting him nicely; he is in great form and he scored his first Test hundred against Australia on Monday. However, a new ball is due and England still need 118 to make Australia bat again.

Sunday, June 11th

After an excellent meal in Ilkley last night I woke to a sunny morning and got a little work done – mainly an article for Kevin Cooper's benefit brochure – before playing golf at Moortown. I started with a birdie four on the first and played quite well for nine holes but then got very wild, once hitting three balls out of bounds on the same hole, one of them proving to be not *my* Ultra four but one of exactly the same type just hit into the middle of our fairway by a member of the foursome coming down the opposite fairway. Of course I had to give him a replacement so I managed in effect to lose four balls on one hole. Ah well, thanks to some doughty work by my partner Jim Thompson we managed to halve the match against John Thicknesse and Stanley Braine, a steady 15-handicapper who made a million-plus in the plastics industry and is now captain of the golfing section of the Forty Club. It was his partner, 'Thickers', however, whose solid five at the last outdid my dumb-headed six (after a near perfect drive) to square the match.

The Australians were enjoying the sunshine and the splendid challenge of Moortown in a separate match behind us. Allan Border and David Boon were first into the bar after us, having also halved their match: a chunky and competitive pair they must be.

Monday, June 12th

England saved the follow-on soon after lunch when Jack Russell off-drove a four which ought to have made his team safe from defeat. But the innings folded not long afterwards and by the close of a hot day Australia had extended that lead to 329. Allan Border was very annoyed when the umpires insisted on taking everyone off three overs early in what seemed to be the first few raindrops of a big storm. In fact, the storm held off.

I am feeling very tired this evening, as I usually do by this stage of a Test. We have no opening windows in our commentary box at Headingley and it gets very stuffy on days like this, aided by F.S.T.'s enormous pipe! The great man is himself looking a bit tired, but every now and again he warms to a theme at the mike and moves the ball all over the place. He is full of the latest piece of absurd internecine warfare in the Yorkshire Club. A new 'Cricket Academy' was launched in style last Wednesday at Bradford, but there is trouble at t'mill because it was suggested in the brochure that first-class cricket *might* return to Bradford (one of Yorkshire's traditional venues, now rather derelict). Some of the Committee object to the very suggestion, thinking Leeds should be the centre of all things pertaining to Yorkshire cricket. So the brochure is going to have to be reprinted.

Tuesday, June 13th

England reserved their worst efforts for the last day. Gower played into the hands of Border and Jones by setting grossly defensive fields at once and, with ample gaps to exploit, the fourth-wicket pair added 72 at seven an over against wayward bowling. A lead of 400 was thus achieved with a minimum of 83 overs to play with.

Thoughtful field-pacing, accurate bowling and fine catching marked the Australian victory which followed. The only luck (and winning sides usually need some of it) came first when Broad was leg before to a creeper from Alderman and then much later when Gooch, the last hope of his side, was given out leg before to a ball which might have missed his leg stump. So often does he work straight balls away to leg off his pads, however, he is bound to suffer occasional dismissals like this, as well as some close decisions in his favour. He hit 10 fours through the attacking fields in the one innings of authority which England could muster.

Whilst Gooch and Barnett were together there was brief talk of a repetition of Headingley 1948, but Barnett, well though he timed the ball again, had already been fortunate to survive a nasty lifter from Hughes before getting caught in a ghastly position, committed to a legside, front-foot shot, by a ball from Alderman which left him and flew from the edge to first slip.

Lawson got Gower in a manner which suggested, I'm afraid, that the England captain still cannot discipline himself to cut out his instinctive strokes when it is essential to do so. He had already almost been caught down the legside by the wicket-keeper; a leg-slip was posted; yet he idly flicked another piece of deliberate bait into Healy's waiting glove. This was not leadership by example, rather deriliction of duty, which is a hard thing to say about so nice a man. It seems to suggest that he still lacks the ability to think deeply about the game, especially in the heat of battle. Sometimes his natural flair will triumph, and gloriously entertain, at others it will seem careless. He *does* care, but he doesn't always think, just like me going down the 18th at Moortown! Let me not condemn him for one lapse, just hope that he and his team will quickly pull themselves together, though I fear this first missed opportunity may have decided the Ashes.

Gower himself is not certain to play next week at Lord's because his damaged right shoulder is hurting him again and he is to have a manipulative operation at the weekend.

Wednesday, June 14th

I drove to Nottingham last night to commentate on today's Benson and Hedges semi-final between Notts and Kent. The Headingley I had left behind had been a deserted, melancholy one. Soon after Australia's triumph it had begun to pour with heavy, thundery rain. I had stayed to do a 'package' (report, interviews and comment) on the match for the 6.45 programme on Radio Two and when I finally got away only two of the dedicated engineering team, led on this occasion by John Devine, had still been there. The ground itself was desolate - grey seats beneath a slate sky. The journey to Southwell, by contrast, was comfortable and pleasant, through mellow country, the rain having been local to Leeds, and a warm welcome awaited me at the Saracen's Head. Unfortunately, however, they gave me a room over the road and, the night being muggy, I woke with a splitting headache which stayed throughout the day.

Nottinghamshire won the game thanks to a decisive spell of bowling by their left-arm spinner, Andy Afford, who was persuaded by Pat Murphy to come up at the end for a live interview on Radio Three. He was down-to-earth, modest and amusing. He only played because of injuries to both the county's overseas players. I hope he will get the just reward of a place in the final against Essex, who beat Somerset in another thrilling finish at Taunton in the other semi-final.

Thursday, June 15th

It was Horsham's turn to field first in hot weather today. Last week, I gather, we had chased 250-odd against Haywards Heath and had begun the last over needing 18 to win. Mark Upton, already 108 not out, required only three balls to finish the match! At one stage he apparently came close to knocking a man painting the pavilion wall off his ladder.

Once again today Jeg, the very shy, emaciated-looking young Horsham groundsman, had produced a superb pitch, spotted with oil from the old grey roller as usual! Mid Surrey declared at 241 for five and after seven days away I felt jaded and out of tune. However, I opened the batting after tea with Craig Ashton from New Zealand and we put on 135 before I was bowled for 63, exhausted, at the start of the last 20 overs. We got the runs, eventually, with only two wickets in hand, our captain for the day, the former Cambridge and Sussex batsman Ian Thwaites, holding himself back to see us home from number ten. Ashton made 83 and has settled very well on this his 'learning' year in England. Tim May of Australia is one of his predecessors as a Horsham guest, but I don't think Ashton is quite Test material. As for the talented Mark Upton, who was on the Sussex staff for two years, this week he hit one straight six then missed his next ball.

Saturday, June 17th

As expected, indeed as almost demanded by the poor performance at Headingley, England will have a fresh attack at Lord's retaining only Foster. Newport was ruled out by injury, Pringle and De Freitas are dropped and into their places come Dilley, Jarvis and the tall fast-medium bowler Angus Fraser who has 37 first-class wickets this season, 32 of them in the Championship at an average of only 18 each. A lumberer in the field, Fraser is, however, a precisely accurate seam bowler who gets bounce from his heght and excellent action. The selectors have kept Emburey in the 12 in the hope that his home ground will bring him badly needed Test wickets – no other spinner has really demanded a place and either Jarvis or Fraser is the likely 12th man.

David Gower is confident that he will be fit despite a manipulative operation on his damaged right shoulder-joint today and his vice-captain Mike Gatting hopes to prove his fitness and form during four days' cricket starting today. Either Barnett or Smith will make way if both Gower and Gatting play.

David Capel is not playing for Northants today because of a slight injury which apparently dissuaded the selectors from picking him at number six and as the fifth bowler despite his brilliant season so far – 34 wickets and just on 600 runs. As a result of the injury to Botham and the reluctance to believe in Capel, England will again lack balance at Lord's.

Wednesday, June 21st

I drove to London in dread of a long wait in traffic jams because of today's national rail strike but in fact the journey took less time than normal. Lord's looked in good order for the second Test starting tomorrow. The pitch has distinct cracks on its surface and in the present hot weather both sides are sure to play a spin bowler.

It is equally crucial to get the fast bowling choice right. It is a common view amongst county cricketers that Paul Jarvis is now the best fast bowler in England so he must play. So, of course, must Dilley, who is an automatic choice when he is fit which is like saying, alas, that Russian cruise liners are the best value when they don't hit icebergs. (One did today.) This leaves Fraser or Foster to drop out. Fraser is a fine young bowler, sensibly chosen for a possible début on his home ground. Foster, by contrast, does not enjoy bowling at Lord's with its disorientating slope across the pitch, but the threat to his place is just the sort of thing to make this fiery young man want to prove a point and, on his day, he is a bowler out of the top drawer. Rather than dent his confidence, therefore, the selectors would be wiser to show faith in Foster.

The batting will depend on decisions made tomorrow about the fitness of Gower, Gatting and Lamb. There now seems serious doubt only about Lamb, who, despite his brilliant first innings hundred at Headingley, appears only 26th on the current list of world batsmen in the Deloittes 'Form Ratings'. Only Gooch (9th) appears in the top ten from the England camp, whereas Australia have four in the top 20, Border (6th), Jones (10th), Waugh (13th), and Boon (18th).

Gooch is very much the man in form, although apparently worried, despite centuries on successive days at Chelmsford, about a fault with his weight falling to the off-side. The best chance England have is to win the toss in sunshine tomorrow and put on 300 plus for very few on the first day. This would be the happiest way of starting their attempt to overcome a poor recent record at Lord's, especially against Australia who have beaten England eight times there this century. England's tally in the same period? One win and one only, after the rain in 1934 when the immaculate Verity, of heroic memory, helped to make Howard Marshall the first of the great cricket commentators.

I stayed with Brian and Pauline Johnston tonight in St John's Wood, 20 minutes walk from Lord's. Bill Frindall and his girl-friend Debbie, a charming school headmistress from Kent, went with us to the Hilton in Park Lane where the Lord's Taverners gave a dinner in honour of the *Test Match Special* commentary team. We were, indeed, honoured. Tim Rice and his brother Jo gave amusing and witty speeches to which the peerless Johnners replied on our behalf. He was, as always, funny and entertaining.

Thursday, June 22nd

It was rather cloudy and cool when I previewed the match from the commentary box at 8.25. I decided to keep for the Radio Three audience the story of Col Stephenson's instructions to the stewards on the eve of the game: "We don't want any more streakers. Keep half an eye on the game but the other half on the crowd. If you see someone about to take her clothes off, jump on her."

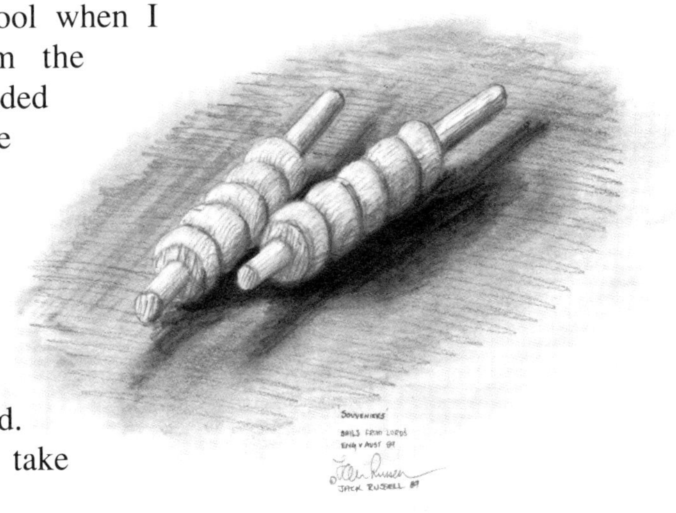

England won the toss but I'm afraid the

batting in the first innings was inadequate. Gower, Gooch and Smith all got going well but none of them stayed to play the big innings as Alderman, Lawson and the very hostile Hughes battled away on a pitch which was lovely for batting once the early greeness had disappeared after lunch.

There was some bad luck and some carelessness as well as some good bowling but it could have been a really dreadful performance if Russell had not batted with perky, plucky good sense. His 64 not out succeeded only, however, in bringing England close to 300 on a pitch which ought to have been worth 450.

Friday, June 23rd

A great day's Test cricket in lovely weather before the second capacity crowd of the match. Nor is there a ticket unsold for tomorrow. Australia were 152 for one shortly before tea, with Taylor and Boon in control despite improved England bowling, but an inspired spell by Foster (two for 43 in 17 overs) pulled England back in the game and Emburey, Dilley and Jarvis took a wicket apiece in an engrossing evening session. Australia are only ten runs behind but the new ball is only one over old, and only Waugh plus the tail remain.

Saturday, June 24th

Black Saturday! Waugh made a brilliant 152 not out. England's bowlers operated from the wrong ends to start with. Australia had all the luck going, punished all the not infrequent bad balls and finished with 528, a lead of 242. Hughes made 30, Hohns 21 and Lawson, if you please, 74.

It got worse. England lost Gooch to the admirable Alderman in the first over, then Barnett and Broad as well. They were a sorry 58 for 3 at the close of play, 184 behind. Can Gatting and Gower emulate May and Cowdrey or Bailey and Watson?

I went to the Saturday evening Press Conference because the man responsible for the interviewing was, reluctantly, obeying the NUJ order for a BBC strike. The brief 'Conference' took place in the marquee on the Lord Harris Garden and when I got there David Gower was being cross-examined by Phil Edmonds (poacher turned gamekeeper) about his field-placings. A hostile battery of microphones and cameras, not to mention reporters' notebooks were pointing at the captain and at Micky Stewart. The captain was planning to leave early for a preview of *Anything Goes*. Suddenly the disappointment and frustration of the day overwhelmed him and he left brusquely and testily. Oh dear: and on Brian Johnston's 77th birthday, too.

Ah well, a day off tomorrow. Everyone involved with the Test match needs a break.

Tuesday, June 27th

Lord's was almost full again yesterday, and the Queen was there for an hour or so. Recriminations and a public rap on the knuckles from Chairman Dexter had followed David Gower's uncharacteristic fall from grace, but happily he restored his public esteem with an innings of immense character. His 15th Test century, and his seventh against

Australia must have been amongst his most satisfying, made as it was with the hounds of hell baying at his heels. One injudicious cut at Hughes followed, perversely, by another the following ball, and one chance to second slip off Alderman when he had made 81 were the only blemishes in an innings memorable not just for the intense atmosphere in which it was compiled but also for the grace and marvellous timing of his strokes.

Gatting, equally determined, had fallen 50 minutes from the start of an engrossing day, once more thrusting out his front pad to a ball moving into his stumps, but into the breach marched Smith, four-square for the cause. He played his best innings for England so far, battling through a torrid spell of short-pitched bowling by Hughes for which, not before time, the bowler was warned for intimidation. Hughes it was, however, who finally broke through when Gower could only fend away to short-leg a short ball which lifted rapidly to his ribs.

This time the captain's example had been magnificent and although Smith, after 208 balls of watchful defiance punctuated by many a masterful stroke, succumbed to a superb away cutter (a match-winning ball?) by Alderman, who followed up by having both Foster and Jarvis leg before, Russell, Emburey and Dilley all made the bowlers sweat. Russell lasted 65 balls, Dilley 64 and Emburey, who had an encouraging match, lasted 96 balls as he and Dilley batted for the first 17 overs today.

Had the thundery shower which fell on Lord's during the lunch interval arrived an hour later, Australia's progress to victory might have been very tense indeed. As it was, some spirited and incisive bowling by Foster denied them their just reward until a few minutes before the start of the last 20 overs. That they made it by six wickets after faltering at 67 for four was due to a confident and authoritative innings by Boon and the cool command of Waugh, though this time he was badly missed in the gully when the total was 91 and the issue not quite resolved.

Wednesday, June 28th

A postscript to the Lord's Test.

England's 'new regime', with Ted Dexter, Micky Stewart and David Gower in the roles of Chairman, Manager and Captain have, between them, had more recent press coverage than their political counterparts in Peking. A small tale from behind the scenes at Lord's may serve to illustrate how seriously they are taking their role, however, and also how little incidents can affect the mass drama of the match itself.

On the third day of the match I was hailed by a prep school cricket master and thanked for signing an autograph or two for some of his charges the previous day. He added that he wished a certain England player had been so polite. He went on to explain that Chris Broad had told one of the boys to **** off. One was very sorry to hear it, of course, but there seemed no reason to doubt the veracity of the story. When, however, the schoolmaster repeated the incident to a well-known cricket correspondent it was immediately passed on to Ted Dexter who cross-examined the player. Broad denied the story completely as Dexter, who was prepared, if necessary, to take disciplinary action, promptly conveyed to the cricket correspondent. He, in turn, rang the schoolmaster and asked him to question the boy again. It eventually transpired that the dishonesty came not from the player but from the boy who, not wishing to be outdone by friends of his who had acquired the autograph in question, whereas he had not, had either invented the whole story or at least substantially embroidered it.

There is more than one moral. Things are not always what they seem at first sight to be. A player's career can depend on more than what he does on the field, especially if he has a 'reputation'. And the image of the side is also dependent on more than just 'visible' matters. Ted Dexter is clearly very concerned about it. Otherwise he would not have gone to the trouble he did to get to the truth of this matter. Terence Rattigan, author of *The Final Test* and *The Winslow Boy*, might have written a play about it!

JULY

Saturday, July 1st

To Horsham this morning to see the start of the Sussex versus Essex match. There was a large crowd, perhaps more than 2,000, and, on this lovely ground with St Mary's Church on one side and the wooded slopes of Denne Hill stretching up above the railway line on the other, there was much more atmosphere than there has been for most Championship matches at Hove in recent years.

Paul Parker went to school in Horsham so it was especially bad luck for him to be unfit to captain due to a persistent hamstring injury. but he saw his team make the running by choosing to field first on a cloudy morning (I wrongly criticised the decision but the superiority and extra pace of county bowlers enabled them to get more out of the pitch than any club bowlers had been able to do) and they bowled Essex out for 185, Dodemaide and Colin Wells (acting captain) taking four wickets each.

I went off at lunchtime to play a second league match of the season for Albury, this time at home against Godalming. I have loved the Albury ground since I first saw it and became involved in helping the club in 1971. Then they were a truly rustic cricket club wanting to replace their old thatched pavilion with something more modern. The replacement we eventually built is a model of its kind, of mellow brick and fitting in neatly with the miles of unspoilt heathland all around.

Since the extraordinary game at Haslemere, Albury have gone from strength to strength and when this match began lay second in the Three Counties League to Aldershot, only four points behind. The only other setback had been defeat in the quarter-final of the Surrey Evening Knockout Cup, the 'Flora Doris' as it is engagingly called after the wives of the competition's two founders. Defeat by Guildford is no disgrace, however. More surprising was that Guildford were then beaten by Farnham in the semi-final despite having both the Surrey Bicknell brothers, Darren and Martin, in their team.

Surrey, like Sussex, are rebuilding at present on a basis of home grown talent and they will be winning county trophies again soon.

WALKER & CO LTD
HORSHAM CC
JACK RUSSELL

Indeed a boy from Farnham, Graham Thorpe, whom I played against in the Flora Doris only a couple of years ago, is one of the best young players in the country. Incidentally, Flora Doris cricket is amongst the most intense I have ever played. Twenty eight-ball overs, often in very poor light, in which every ball counts. My original club, before we moved house to Albury, was Cranleigh and I had the fun of playing for 'Cup Final' winning teams for both Cranleigh (helped then by the Cranleigh schoolmaster, ex Oxford and Notts, Andy Corran) and Albury. There is a particular satisfaction when relatively small clubs like these can humble the likes of Farnham and Guildford where the majority of the best players have congregated since league cricket came south.

Today Albury were too good for Godalming. Another itinerant Kiwi, David Watson, hit a brilliant, hard-hitting 125 on a very dry and rather unreliable pitch and we declared at 202 for five, then bowled them out with five overs in hand, well led by Martin Smith who was still flushed from having made 58 the previous week when Tonbridge successfully chased 290 to win against Downside in The Cricketer Cup.

I had a bug and was happy to go in at six today and make 10 not out before the declaration. I forgot my diarrhoea and sore throat during an enjoyable and slightly unluckly bowl but Jeff Austin and Mike Gore took the wickets. This time there was no needle or nastiness, I am glad to say. Especially so, in fact, because only a few days ago I was talking to a regular club umpire, Reg Wilderspin from Nutfield, who told me that, quite without provocation or cause, he had been rudely asked if he knew the laws of cricket by an MCC cricketer at Abinger who, a few minutes before, at the start of the game, had greeted him as an old friend! At issue was whether or not he should have allowed a couple of leg byes in, if you please, a Sunday afternoon friendly match. Cricket is lost if we abandon courtesy between player and player or umpire and player.

Sunday, July 2nd

I couldn't eat today with some nasty summer bug warming up inside, but still had to report and comment on the Test team for Edgbaston which was predictable enough, apart from the dropping of Chris Broad and the retention of Kim Barnett, to whom the Australians would rather bowl, I'm sure, then Broad. The Derbyshire captain saved his bacon with a fighting hundred for his county yesterday and the question of whether or not Ian Botham, now fit again, should return was settled by his taking six wickets for Worcestershire against Northants, especially as one of his victims was Capel, beaten by three balls and caught off the fourth.

Fraser will definitely play this time, taking over from Jarvis, who is unlucky. Dilley, as usual, is doubtful because of fitness. I don't think he was really fit for Lord's and it may be a blessing in disguise if both Fraser and Jarvis play in support of Foster.

Monday, July 3rd

I left *The Cricketer* office in time to see Sussex taking what looks like being a winning hold on their match with Essex during the third session on a gloriously sunny evening. There had been 6,000 to watch the Sunday League match yesterday and there were 2,000 plus today so John Dew and the Horsham committee are all delighted. What is more, the players of both sides are praising an ideal cricket wicket, with much more pace and bounce in it than most. Well done Jeg!

If Sussex do win tomorrow it will be a triumph for a youngish side gradually finding its feet and insisting on playing at least one of their two leg-spinners, Andy Clarke and Ian Salisbury, in every match. Essex are currently leading the Championship and the Sunday League and will be at Lord's for the B and H Final in a fortnight. However, Gooch is not at his best at present, Mark Waugh, Steve's twin brother, has been inconsistent, Pringle is not very fit and Foster is looking rather a disgruntled character at the moment. I am told that he has been tackling journalists about what they have written about him, which may be understandable and is no doubt often justified, but which will, alas, do him no good. I sympathise with him. Only the other day a newspaper article claimed that I earn far more that I actually do from after-dinner speaking and very annoying indeed it is to have a falsity printed about one. But Neil would be wiser to do his talking through good, hostile, accurate bowling.

What Foster and others must accept is that although the boys from Wapping may seem to relish criticising the England team they would much prefer to be writing happy stories of success.

Wednesday, July 5th

I drove to Birmingham this morning with the Sevenoaks bookseller Martin Wood as my passenger because of the train strike which now, it seems, has become a regular Wednesday feature of British life. Martin is handicapped but runs a successful small business selling second-hand cricket books. He is to be seen at every Test match and usually has some strong, sometimes mildly eccentric view to impart.

When I arrived at the ground England's problems were multiplying fast. David Gower had been given the option of not talking to the press by the TCCB but wisely did so. He knows that continued failure will not be forgiven but he knows also that it is important to keep the writers happy, ignorant though he may feel some of them to be. When he chatted outside the players' dining room on a sunny afternoon, three of his selected

THE TWIN TOWERS, TAUNT
© JACK RUSSELL '89

12 were already out of the match (Foster, finger blister; Lamb, shoulder; Smith, hamstring) and even as he spoke Mike Gatting was leaving the ground having just heard that his wife's mother had died. Chris Tavare was hastily traced to Taunton by Ted Dexter and summoned to resume his Test career after a five year break.

I drove to the Belfry after delivering a fairly pessimistic preview of the game from Pebble Mill studios, including intervews with Gower and the personable, intelligent and level-headed Tim Curtis, whose own call-up came yesterday.

It was a lovely, warm, summery evening and there was time for nine holes on the Derby Course with John Thicknesse. The Ryder Cup will be contested in two months' time over the neighbouring Brabazon course, which looks in really splendid condition.

Thursday, July 6th

England would probably have settled for a draw before a ball of the Edgbaston Test had been bowled. As it happened they were already fighting an uphill battle when an almighty storm broke over the ground on this first evening. Australia made 232 for four after winning the toss. Jones is 71 not out and he batted with his usual enterprise, tempered by excellent judgement of when to attack and when to leave the ball alone. Such is his appetite for runs he will probably one day score a 300 in a Test.

He came in when Australia were in a bit of trouble: Taylor and Marsh had launched the innings purposefully but some canny bowling by Emburey and Botham, England's most experienced bowlers, pegged them down less comfortably. Taylor was stumped off a ball which turned substantially past his off-stump, Marsh was lbw driving at a ball of full length and then Border made a strange misjudgement and was bowled playing no shot.

Australia had thus lost three wickets for 17 runs, but the return of Dilley enabled Jones and Boon to launch a recovery and although Fraser and Emburey restored England's control the only other wicket of the day came from sheer fortune when Jarvis deflected a fierce straight drive onto the stumps, leaving the unlucky Boon stranded. It was, at least, a good bit of fielding by Jarvis who is a better cricketer than he has generally shown himself to be in the two Tests he has played this season but who will only prove it if he allows

his brain to control his heart.

I was broadcasting in the open air when the storm broke and I got thoroughly soaked. The road outside the ground was flooded but the water had subsided a bit by the time that I drove up to Bernard Thomas's famous Physiotherapy Clinic where, as is traditional during the Birmingham Test, he was hosting a party on behalf of the sporting folk of the area. As usual there was convivial company and the wine and cheese went down well.

Friday, July 7th

There was a long, long wait today for the rain to stop. The ground looked rather dreary and miserable, black plastic covering more than half of its turf, but the crowd were marvellously cheerful and as tuneful as a Welsh choir when they broke out with a chorus of 'Singing In The Rain'.

Thanks to 'Brumbrella', which protected the square despite the fracture of the steel drum off which it is rolled, 15 overs were possible on this second day and there was some sparkling cricket for these patient souls to enjoy in the late afternoon. Given his chance with the new ball Fraser confirmed his arrival by becoming the first man to get Waugh out in the series, hitting his off stump with a ball which nipped back through a forward push, although not before Waugh had played some scintillating strokes, mainly at the expense of Dilley. Fraser also ripped one back through Healy's slightly crooked defence but Jones took full toll of a succession of long hops and half volleys to reach his hundred off 160 balls with 11 fours.

Saturday, July 8th

Australia finally locked England out of the game during just over two hours of play before a disappointed capacity crowd who saw Dilley having Hughes caught at second slip in the first of two sessions punctuated by drizzle. Even though conditions were moist and sultry, ideal for swing bowling, dogged batting by Hohns, who ought to be a couple of places higher in what is, despite its meritorious achievements, an extremely vulnerable Australian tail, frustrated England for the rest of the day. Although the ball was still hard and new, Gower failed to pressurise the batsmen with attacking fields and when Hohns did edge the luckless Jarvis to second slip, Botham this time could not cling on. Jones simply batted on.

Sunday, July 9th

I am writing this with considerable difficulty on my Hitachi PC HL320, having possibly broken my thumb in successful defence today of the Benson and Hedges Ash! This is traditionally contested between the England and Australia media teams on the rest day of a Test match and in view of my ignominy today I feel I should record that I have at home a bronze medal, one of B and H Australia's genuine man of the match medals, presented for making 57 and taking 3 for 23 in our last match in Sydney.

Keen to repeat the performance today on a grey afternoon and a suet pudding of a pitch at the West Warwicks ground at Olton in South

Birmingham, I stopped a savage drive off one of my own full tosses early in the Australian innings and felt a sharp pain. I thought it was a bad bruise and carried on bowling with reasonable success but as soon as I got a bat in my hand I knew it might be a broken bone.

Stupidly I went out to bat and felt a shock of pain when glancing my second ball for four. Even more stupidly, I did not retire hurt and was bowled by Martin Blake's next ball. Insult was added to injury because this ball was captured by Channel 10 Television, present at the match for its novelty value, and was beamed throughout Australia a few hours later with no mention of my incapacity! England won, thanks to a doughty stand between Derek Seymour (ITV) and Peter Hayter (Mail On Sunday) following useful knocks by Brian Scovell (Daily Mail), John Etheridge (Sun) and David Munden (photographer, ex-Leicestershire and Young England). The former Test off-spinner Keith Slater and the left-arm spinner Mark Ray of Tasmania were successfully kept at bay. I stayed for a few drinks with my thumb wrapped in ice but I shall ask for an X-ray tomorrow, just in case.

Monday, July 10th

I rang Bernard Thomas this morning and he kindly organised the X-ray. Sure enough I have a bad break at the base of the thumb and I had the hand wrapped in plaster this evening at the Nuffield hospital next door to Bernie's clinic. (I was treated by Mr Tubbs, an orthopaedic surgeon of renown who recently did Graham Dilley's knee and tells me Dilley has shown great character to come back to play so swiftly.) I shall have this hand in plaster for four weeks. Bang goes cricket and golf for that period – and we are due in Devon next week for a family holiday based on golf! Ah well, it could have been the right hand.

I also feel the good Lord had arranged for me to renew my acquaintance with Bernard Thomas only two days before the accident. As he always was in the past he was both sympathetic and efficient. He deserves his success. They say he drives the only privately owned Rolls Royce in Birmingham!

The sunshine returned after the weekend and England, having finally finished the job after Border had decided to bat on, subsided unbelievably to 75 for five. Alderman took two for 29 in a marvellously controlled opening spell of 13 overs, having a bamboozled Gower lbw with an inswinger after beating his outside edge frequently, then getting Tavare at first slip. Gooch had already been lbw for the fourth time in five innings and by teatime Curtis and Barnett had also departed. Curtis had at least hit, seven fours, amongst them some crisply timed cuts and also a hook off Hughes, whose verbal aggression was blatant and unpleasant. He still got his man, however, and followed up later in the day by bowling Botham with a straight half-volley to end his face-saving sixth wicket stand with Russell.

Putting on 96, Botham and Russell simply played sound, orthodox cricket but when Russell was caught at slip off a leg-spinner that bounced more than he had expected, only a few minutes after Botham's quite unexpected missed drive, the air of crisis returned.

Tuesday, July 11th

England needed 40 with three wickets in hand to save the follow-on when the last day began and got there with a straight drive by Jarvis with the last pair together. Fraser ran himself out in the first over but Emburey and Jarvis played some brave shots through attacking fields and Dilley defended stoutly.

Border decided there was no time to make a declaration so Taylor was given time to make another attractive 50 his fourth in six innings in the series, Marsh repeated his first innings 42 and Boon and Headley got batting practice. Botham took a brilliant slip catch to give Gooch, who bowled well, a rare Test wicket and Jarvis at last hit the stumps. But there was not much to console England, nor me as I drove cautiously back down the motorway with only one hand on the wheel. Thank goodness my car has automatic transmission!

Wednesday, July 12th

The cricket season gets hectic hereabouts. Today was the NatWest second round day. I saw Sussex score 300 for two against Leicestershire, with Paul Parker and Alan Wells both making undefeated 80s. Their efforts were matched by Peter Willey but not by the other Leicestershire batsmen against brilliant, committed fielding. The other winners were Lancashire (off the last ball at Bristol), Middlesex, Surrey, Warwickshire, Hampshire, Worcestershire and Northants. The eventual winners may be one of the last two named there. Worcester are returning to form and Northants, who have slipped a long way behind Essex in the Championship, must surely win something this year.

Thursday, July 13th

There was a press conference at Lord's today after the ICC meeting. They have appointed Colin Cowdrey to be chairman and roving ambassador for the next four years but most of their decisions were negative: no immediate action on an international panel of umpires; no Test status for Zimbabwe; no audience for the South Africans; and no restrictions on bouncers.

James played for Horsham in my stead today and was top-scorer with an excellent 51 in an exciting draw against Stanmore. Angus Fraser, a pillar of Stanmore, has played in this fixture several times in the past so although they had no-one of his class bowling against him today, James had every reason to be pleased with himself. He was the youngest player in the game but Stanmore's most effective batsman, who also kept wicket as well, was a woman, Sandra Trott, from New Zealand. She and her husband, Murray, have played host to various Stanmore cricketers in Wellington, the Fraser brothers included.

I watched some of the match before broadcasting from the Horsham studio about the ICC meeting at Lord's. It was never very likely that the TCCB attempt to reduce the permissible number of bouncers to one an over would be voted into the laws. That a majority of the Test-playing countries opted for the proposal, which was seconded by New Zealand, does, however, give some hope that the crucial battle to preserve a proper balance in cricket between subtle skills on one hand and the tactics of fear and blood on the other may eventually be won.

One or two of the associate member nations – who really ought not to have been voting at all on a matter which did not directly concern them – may have voted with the West Indies for reasons of some misguided notion of political solidarity: the Third World sticking together as it were, which in cricketing terms is nonsense. Others may have felt that one bouncer an over is leaning too far towards making life easy for the batsman or even that the TCCB's proposal did not seek to define what a bouncer is. The Australians have used an adequate definition for their limited-overs matches of 'a ball which bounces over the shoulders of a batsman standing in his normal stance.' Admittedly this is not perfect because the normal stance of men such as Sunil Gavaskar or Harry Pilling is somewhat different in height from that of Angus Fraser or Curtley Ambrose. But one must assume some degree of intelligence and common sense on the part of Test match umpires.

Everyone understands why the West Indies do not wish to see any further restriction on the amount of bouncers bowled. They have an apparent unceasing supply of tall and powerful fast bowlers and they have discovered that with four such men bowling the vast majority of their overs they are guaranteed to win any given Test series of more than three matches, because on most pitches the fast bowlers will eventually get their man. Only when the West Indies are given a taste of their own medicine – i.e. four fast bowlers of similar accuracy and strength, with other bowlers of equal speed and skill in reserve – will that situation change.

The West Indies are, however, in a minority of one in their wish to maintain the status quo and have no limit on the number of bouncers bowled except when they amount to intimidation. The total inadequacy of this law is self-evident. Only once has a bowler been taken off in a Test because of it, yet the number of batsmen hit and hurt is very considerable.

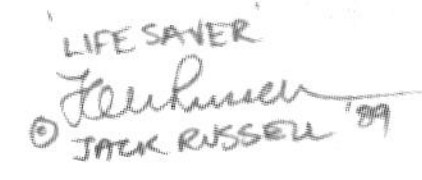

Friday, July 14th

I was due to preview the Benson and Hedges Cup Final from Lord's thisafternoon, but the BBC went on strike, and this gave me a bit more time to catch up with a mountain of letters at home. I did nip in to Broadcasting House to record something just in case, before driving down to the Embankment for a cheery cocktail party given by the Cricket Society (of which I am a life member) on the RS *Hispaniola.* It was extremely hot, however, and my plastered left arm is very uncomfortable in this steamy weather.

Brian Johnston kindly put me up for the night in St John's Wood because I have to be at Lord's early for a *Today* broadcast in the morning. Brian's wife Pauline is visiting relatives in Canada and my brood has left today for a week in a rented house on the edge of Thurlestone Golf Course. Touch wood, I shall join them tomorrow night.

Saturday, July 15th

A marvellous B and H final, especially for all connected with Nottinghamshire, who beat Essex by three wickets when Eddie Hemmings, needing four off the last ball, achieved exactly that by square-driving a perfectly placed last delivery from J.K. Lever. Two 40 year olds showing their quality in a game designed for the young! It was a beautiful day as far as the weather was concerned and a great game of limited-overs cricket with Alan Lilley making the highest score and Tim Robinson batting better than anyone. This was a happy note on which to drive to Devon for a badly needed five day break, although one could not help feeling sorry for Essex who have now lost four B and H finals since winning their first one in 1979.

Sunday, July 23rd

Tim Robinson's reward for his fine innings last week and, more significantly, his excellent form all season, was a recall to the Test 12 with Nick Cook preferred to John Childs as Emburey's spinning partner. Those left out, all too predictably, are Jarvis, Barnett and Tavare. Lamb is unfit for the third time for a third different reason – this time, poor chap, a broken finger. But Smith is back and thank goodness for that. He may be joined by several other younger players if England don't manage to turn the tide this time but the selectors are probably right to stick with the players they know, at least until the Ashes have been lost.

Tuesday, July 25th

Essex were today penalised 25 Championship points because of an unsatisfactory pitch at Southend for their match against Yorkshire. The unprecedented decision means that they both have lost three points from their ninth victory, instead of gaining 22. The board's statement condemned the Southchurch Park pitch at Southend as 'Not properly prepared and clearly unsuitable for first-class cricket'. They stressed that there was no question of *deliberate* under-preparation of the pitch by Essex.

The panel who made the decision, three of them after watching every ball of Essex's victory, comprised Donald Carr, Tim Lamb, Alan Smith and Ossie Wheatley of the TCCB, with Ken Taylor the Notts manager as the neutral observer. The decision will reverberate through county cricket. It does more than merely open up the Championship, which was starting to look like Nashwan versus the rest.

Ironically, two of the main beneficiaries are Worcestershire and Northamptonshire, both of whom in the last two years have produced pitches which have had their visitors grumbling.

Essex will consider it doubly unfortunate that the condemned pitch is not their main one at Chelmsford but one of several grounds on which they play very profitably for a week each year as a deliberate policy of taking their attractive, successful side around the county, keeping both members and sponsors happy. Southend is in any case likely to be one of many casualties if the TCCB decide this winter to move to a Championship programme of 16 four-day games.

But if this does happen, it is absolutely essential that pitches should be satisfactory – starting firm, dry and true with an even growth of grass to allow a bit of pace for the use of the best bowlers and batsmen and starting to wear on the third day to give spinners their chance. Nothing is more important than good pitches if England's Test fortunes are to revive.

As for the justice of this Southend decision, having decided on a new rule for this season the Board had to apply it. Essex were possibly fortunate to get away with it after the first match at Southend last week when they won on a pitch which the umpires also deemed to be unsatisfactory. The recent drought conditions and the fact that Essex do not have full control over grounds they don't own were mitigating factorsbut this was a necessary decision *pour encourager les autres.*

On the Test front the news that the unfortunate Graham Dilley's knee is injured again is further bad luck for England – but it also makes the selectors decision straightforward – they will play the remaining eleven and no doubt call up Paul Jarvis as 12th man.

Thursday, July 27th

England, having established that poor Graham Dilley was unfit with water on the knee again, left out his replacement, Jarvis, prior to winning the toss. At the end of the first day against an unchanged Australia on a dry pitch of easy pace but uneven bounce they are 224 for seven, owing almost everything to Robin Smith's accomplished and often brilliant batting. He is 112 not out but Lawson with the first three wickets (four in all) and Hohns, whose three wickets included Gower and Botham in quick succession, both bowled exceptionally well. It was a most disappointing performance by England again but thanks to a spirited and sensible innings by Foster, whose straight six off Hohns was the shot of the day, they are not necessarily out of this match after one day as they more or less have been in the first three games of the rubber.

Friday, July 28th

Oh, dear. Another grim day for England I'm afraid, and the hounds are out for Gower's blood again. Smith added 31 more to finish with 143 out of 260, a gem set in a ring of barbed wire.

I have myself unintentionally caused a bit of a stir by mentioning Terry Alderman's habit of dousing his lips with 'block-out' sun cream and then licking his lips as he walks back with the ball. I suggested to Robin Jackman, who is summarising with Fred Trueman in this match, that it is against Law 42 artificially to interfere with the condition of the ball and that it must be difficult for Alderman not to apply some of the grease to the ball, albeit inadvertently. I suppose, if I am honest with myself, that I was by implication expressing suspicion over the need for Terry to put cream on when the weather is cool and cloudy. But Australians have to worry about skin cancer which most English people do not. Unfortunately it was picked up by a few papers here and several in Australia. I certainly didn't want to cause trouble for Terry, who is much liked and respected.

Lawrie Sawle, the charming Australian manager, and Bobby Simpson, his wordly-wise team coach, whose planning has had much to do with the Australian success, listened to the tape today in the control room behind our commentary box on the roof of the building at the Stretford End. They were very friendly and sensible about it. After close of play I drove to Liverpool to have dinner and spend the night with the

Bishop, David Sheppard and his wife Grace. I felt very privileged to be having a delicious kitchen supper in such distinguished yet modest and homely company. The Bishop's Lodge is an imposing Victorian house in a fashionable residential area with a commanding view, taking in some of Liverpool's less salubrious areas.

We walked in their lovely garden before eating and they talked about the changes they have made to it in their 14 years in residence, as well as discussing cricket, the Church, problems in the Diocese and the immensly busy life they lead. The main purpose of the visit, however, was to exchange views on South Africa. David Sheppard has been a brave campaigner against *apartheid* but had never been to the country until a visit in May with his close friend Bishop Warlock. They saw much of the nasty side of life in the townships which is hidden to most visitors. They showed me an excellent album of photographs well named 'Black hope, White fear'. I have written much about South African cricket but we all know it is only a small part of the greater problem. *Apartheid* has to go and it is a question now only of whether men of good will can outlaw the extremists on either side, especially, of course, the hard-liners in, or to the right of, the Nationalist Government.

Saturday, July 29th

A satisfactory day for me. It began with invigorating morning prayers in the Bishop's private Chapel. England had a slightly better day, even though they ended it 181 behind with one more wicket still to take (Border, Jones and Waugh all played with immense determination to turn the last screw). I had some enjoyable conversations with my blind friend, Mike Howell, who follows cricket on the radio with such dedication and who has such a marvellously cheerful approach to life. Then, after play, I had a friendly chat with Terry Alderman to apologise for my causing him some unwanted headlines, and later I made a generously received speech in aid of Lancashire's Pavilion Restoration Fund.

Sunday, July 30th

Quite a lot of rain fell today, at least in Cheshire where I am staying, as usual, at The Swan. Brian Johnston and I were royally entertained by Donald and Izza Kenyon at their lovley house near Knutsford. Donald's firm supplies covers to all but four of the main county grounds, not to mention Wimbledon, Twickenham (frost protection) and many other great sporting venues. His balloon cover was keeping the rain off the square at Old Trafford even as we tucked into our roast beef at his family home.

Monday, July 31st

A desperate day for England left Australia within four wickets of the Ashes with only the rain and Jack Russell to worry about. The wizard of the pencil hung on gamely with John Emburey until rain arrived before the scheduled close, by which time Alderman had reduced England to an unbelievable 59 for six.

When I got back to The Swan at Bucklow Hill, various straws in the wind suggested that the 'South African Story' on which I have been quite well informed, might be about to break. I have known for some time that a tour was more or less certain this winter – most people in fact have guessed as much and had a shrewd idea of several players who had signed to go on two tours of South Africa in the next two winters. However, not until checking with various sources tonight did I finally cross most of the t's and dot the i's. Originally the SACU did not want to release the names until the end of the season, so as not to disrupt the Ashes series.

No-one will know, incidentally, how much a preoccupation with deciding whether to accept offers of more than £80,000 for each tour, tax paid, has affected the performances of the men in the proposed tour party, eight of whom have played against Australia this season. A ninth player, Mike Gatting, is apparently close to signing but the possibility of regaining the England captaincy *might* dissuade him.

When I spoke to a source in South Africa this morning the plan had been to release the names this coming Thursday, because the tabloid newspaper *Today* has been close to getting the correct details. When the first editions of the Tuesday newspapers came off the presses at about ten o'clock this evening it was clear that *Today* had almost cracked the entire story, so I got in touch with the BBC and recorded pieces for the midnight news telling all that I could without breaking any confidences with my main sources in South Africa and England. I got to bed at one o'clock and set my alarm for 5.45!

August

Tuesday, August 1st

This was such a momentous day that it is difficult to know where to begin. The South African Story was spreading fast and I was at Old Trafford by a quarter to seven to service various morning programmes.

One of them was intended to be *Breakfast Time* but the taxi supposed to take me to Piccadilly Studio in Manchester did not show up – or at least missed me whilst I waited by the main gates after talking to the *Today* programme on Radio Four. Instead of the taxi I saw Jack Russell driving in and greeted him with a good luck message and an imprecation to bat all day. Cheery as ever he said he would do his best although the wicket was turning. He was in the nets by half-past nine and by heavens he would have batted all day if he had not run out of partners. Neat, perky, brave and determined, he defied the Australian bowlers until half-past three: a quite heroic innings of 128 not out. It was not only his first Test hundred but his first in first-class cricket. This was the real stuff of dreams and Test history and it almost seemed that Russell and Emburey would go down alongside Bailey and Watson, and May and Cowdrey, in the folklore of the game. But Alderman broke through in the afternoon to bowl Emburey after a characteristically defiant 64 in his final Test innings.

So a brighter complexion was put on England's third defeat in four Tests this season and

David Gower was able to announce, almost with a smile, that he will soldier on for at least two more Tests. The odds are that Gower, Gooch or Botham will take England to the West Indies in January and that England will then lose again.

To be cold-hearted about it, the three are expendable and the captain in the West Indies needs to be that. The alternative is a senior county player like Parker, Nicholas or Roebuck, but there is a need these days for Test captains to be groomed for the job and the Cambridge and Lancashire batsman Mike Atherton seems to me to be the man who should be prepared for a long term appointment as soon as possible. He has captained cricket teams since early boyhood, is widely respected, a mature batsman of the necessary class and a useful leg-break bowler. But his job will be much easier if he is taken on tour and given top level experience as early as possible.

Australia have thoroughly and indisputably deserved their triumph. At last they have become a successful side under the durable Allan Border. Never has any Test captain worked harder for success. Seldom has anyone shown such loyalty and patience as Lawrie Sawle, chairman of Australia's selectors through the dark years and, as manager, the unsung hero of this tour.

Prior to this tour Border had captained Australia in 39 Tests and won only seven of them: 13 were lost, one tied and the rest drawn. His own batting never faltered until last winter when the West Indies bowlers finally sorted him out. But although the press called him 'Grumpy' at one stage he did not give up. The reward for him and for Australia's streetwise and thorough manager, Bobby Simson, is great indeed. Border is the first Australian captain to regain, as opposed to retain, the Ashes in England since Bill Woodfull in 1934.

England now have no option but to rebuild their team, a necessity strengthened by the fact that nine of those who have played against Australia this season – Gatting, Barnett, Foster, Dilley, Jarvis, DeFreitas, Emburey, Broad and Robinson – are all in the unofficial touring party of 16 to South Africa. Most of the players will be paid a little under £85,000 plus tax for two tours, the first taking place next year between late January and early March. They will be banned from international cricket for five years from the date of their last departure from South Africa, assuming the new chairman of ICC, Colin Cowdrey, accepts them back. One of those on whom he will have to adjudicate is his own son. Incidentally although attempts will be made to involve the players in some way in cricket in the black townships, community leaders there are sure to oppose the idea and there will be recriminations from anti-*apartheid* groups even though the SACU will claim that they need the tours to keep first-class cricket going in South Africa and to raise further funds for the development programme.

In some ways the departure of the disillusioned 16 makes it easier for England to rebuild. In the fast bowling department, however, the cupboard will be left very bare. Angus Fraser finds himself first choice after two Test matches. The only other young fast bowlers in serious contention are Steve Watkin and Martin Bicknell: after that the choice will have to come from Small, Cowans, Agnew and Radford, with the injured Newport returning to contention for the West Indies tour.

England could yet send a reasonably experienced batting side to West Indies based around Gower, Botham, Gooch, Lamb and Robin Smith but the last two Tests of this summer must be used to blood one or two others against Australia's less than fearsome attack. Nasser Hussain has still not gone in higher than five for Essex but he seems to have climbed above Mark Ramprakash and Michael Atherton from that generation. There is a middle-twenties group, however, whose chances have been limited or non-existent. They include Bailey, Capel, Benson, Chris Smith, John Morris and Whitaker. Needless to say the choice of spinners is depressingly small. Child stands out as the best of the experienced ones, and Medlycott and Afford of the younger left-armers but the only off-spinners under 30 playing regular first-class cricket are the unsung Pierson of Warwickshire and Trump of Somerset.

Ted Dexter yesturday admitted the need to rebuild the team but whether the TCCB will decide to make more fundamental changes to English cricket remains to be seen.

Wednesday, August 2nd

Off to Lord's to commentate on the Middlesex versus Sussex quarter-final in the NatWest trophy, although my route took me via Horsham where I did a live two-way with Julian Tutt (a *TMS* commentator of the future?) for the *Today* programme. How I should have liked a decent night's sleep instead of the early start! I had only got home, with a headache, at 11.30 the previous evening.

One suggestion put to me was that people no longer want to play for England as much as they did. I think that is rubbish, certainly for younger players. For the ones who have played in many Tests and have their tax-free benefits behind them, I suppose it might be true, however. They play rather too much high-pressure cricket, even for professionals.

Middlesex qualified fairly easily for the semi-final of the NatWest. Mike Gatting looked like a man with no cares as he hit a commanding hundred and shared a big stand with Desmond Haynes and John Emburey, another of the departing stars, then exploited a worn wicket (it had been used for the previous Championship match) with some brilliant bowling. It is such a shame that he is bowling so well now that he has turned his back on England, having striven in vain for his form for so long, mainly because of his insistence on having close fielders when the ball has not been turning. It certainly did today, however, and Paul Parker, whom I found quietly fuming on the stairs beside the Sussex dressing room after the match, was annoyed that a new pitch had not been offered. Middlesex had shared their misgivings before the match, but Lord's is, of course, under MCC's jurisdiction, not their own.

There was yet another late departure from a cricket ground for me because after the game Mike Gatting gave a press conference in the Banqueting Suite. He was a little out of his depth when it came to a cross-examination on political matters. His prime motive, he said, was the future financial security of his family, although he had decided to go only last Tuesday morning before discussing money. He is obviously thoroughly disillusioned by the collapse of his Test career since its high point of 1985-86 but he will surely have times in the next seven years when he wishes he could be playing for his country again.

The other successful counties today were Warwickshire, Worcestershire and Hampshire.

Sunday, August 6th

Despite choosing two new caps, a situation more or less forced on them, Ted Dexter, David Gower and Micky Stewart managed a remarkably conservative choicc for this week's fifth Test at Trent Bridge in a situation demanding radicalism.

They had fallen between the stools of planning ahead and of trying to find a way of beating Australia in a series already lost. Even so the five men who have not played in the series before - Atherton, Malcolm, Moxon, Hemmings and Thomas - brings the number of England players in the series so far to 26, only two fewer than last year when Peter May and his fellow selectors were villified for chopping and changing too much. In both years, of course, injuries have been unusually prevalent and the reason for Greg Thomas's sudden appearance in the 12 was the withdrawal yesterday of Gladstone Small with a strain. Thomas was a significant absentee, in view of the fact that he has spent several successful winters in South Africa, from the 16 'defectors' named last week. He is lucky, however, to be preferred to Norman Cowans or to younger challengers like Bicknell and his fellow Welshman Watkin.

The unofficial tour has, incidentally, been greeted with extraordinary hysteria considering that everyone knew a tour was bound to take place and that the ICC Agreement in January was specifically designed to solve the problem when it arose.

Atherton's leadership experience no doubt won him preference in this case ahead of Nasser Hussain, the brilliantly gifted Durham and Essex batsman, but if the choice was between the two of them, Hussain was clearly the form horse. He has scored two first-class hundreds for Essex since coming down from Durham and has been habitually their highest scorer on all sorts of wickets. It looks as though Atherton, Hussain and Ramprakash are going to pull ahead of a lost middle generation which includes John Morris, James Whitaker and Rob Bailey, who made a late decision not to go to South Africa. But the selectors must beware of sending too many youngbloods to the West Indies: not that they will be tempted to if Gower and Stewart have anything to do with it! Devon Malcolm was born in Jamaica, came to England as a 16 year old and originally played for Derbyshire as an overseas player. With his glasses he has the look of a scholar but he is immensely strong and bowls a cricket ball very fast and increasingly accurately, although he still has much to learn. This season however he has done as well as his two West Indies Test team-mates at Derby, Michael Holding and Ian Bishop, and along with a fit David Lawrence he might be capable of matching fire with fire in the Caribbean next year.

The selection of the spinners and the opening batsman are really disappointing. It is a pity, in view of Cook's modest performance and negative approach at Old Trafford that a gamble has not been taken with Keith Medlycott. He emphasised his skill, sadly a few days too late, by taking seven wickets at The Oval on Monday. One expects little, I'm afraid, of Hemmings and less of Cook so perhaps Medlycott will get his chance for the last game on his home ground. Hemmings has taken 16 Test wickets for England at 54 each: he is a worthy fellow and a dedicated professional cricketer but, on his home ground or not, a dubious selection in present circumstances.

The opening partnership of Curtis and Moxon does not inspire much confidence with 13 Tests between them but both know how to build an innings. The selectors say they discussed the position with Graham Gooch who was unhappy with his form, but his apparent willingness to relinquish his place temporarily (and the £2050 fee which in his case goes with it) has something to do, perhaps, with his desire to help Essex to maintain their challenge in the two main county competitions.

Wednesday, August 9th

How different driving to Nottingham this time. The green and pleasant land has turned a rather sickly yellow, some fields almost the colour of log-ash. The drought has become worrying in some places, although the cricket fields are not yet all as brown and burnt as they were in 1976. On some of them the pitches have become too dry and the top surfaces have started to go, giving bowlers a chance for revenge for all the pastings they have taken from batsmen throughout the summer, in club and village cricket if not in the county game where very few batsmen have enjoyed really consistent success.

Most of the exceptions come, I'm afraid from overseas. Jimmy Cook, who has quietly been one of the best players in the world for several years now, has come to Somerset at the age of 36 and played wonderfully well with his sound basic technique. He has also proved an ideal ambassador for his country. It is one of the many injustices of *apartheid* and the hatred of it shared by all except the Government which still applies it, that many admirable men and women get tarred with the brush. Since last week there has been much talk, as there was at the time of the 'defections' of English players to World Series Cricket, about the rates of pay available to county and Test cricketers.

Phillip DeFreitas dreaming of home

Some despise those who said yes to the offer of a contract in South Africa because they see the tours, rightly or wrongly, as being fortifying to the South African Government.

The pressure of the opposition to the tour finally persuaded the two 'non-white' members, Philip DeFreitas and Roland Butcher, to drop out yesterday, in Butcher's case a considerable financial sacrifice, because he has no chance of resuming his brief England career. Both men had received some vicious 'hate' mail. (This does not surprise me because I received a letter threatening my life before I went to the West Indies three years ago, presumably for being prepared to speak up for South African *cricket*, though I would never have done so if I thought it would help *apartheid*. I happen to believe that the extremists of both sides place a much greater importance on cricket in South Africa than is realistic. So, in fact, do the media. The decisions by Butcher and DeFreitas that all the unpleasantness simply was not going to be worth the money hardly seemed worthy of front-page banner headlines, but that is what they got.)

The majority of county cricketers seem to be saying 'Good luck' to the 'rebels'. They have taken a perfectly legitimate career decision. It certainly sticks in the throat, however, that the 'signing on' had to be done behind closed doors. If they had been open about their interest in South Africa they would be less open to criticism.

Opportunity certainly hammers at the door of those who remain, and although the selectors should have been bolder with their selections for the Trent Bridge Test which starts tomorrow, the loss of the Ashes is compensated to some extent by interest in the performances of the two new caps, Michael Atherton and Devon Malcolm. It is a pity Medlycott is not playing in place of Cook, Capel instead of Botham and, perhaps, Hussain in place of Atherton, since the latter has not actually been in anything like such impressive form.

Most of the professionals would disagree, because they all tend to be cautious and conservative. This is the trouble with the Gower/Stewart combination: they both tend to go for players they know. Talking this evening at the Saracen's Head in Southwell to some of the Essex second XI players, who are staying there during their match with Notts at

Newark, there seemed to be a general feeling amongst the likes of Keith Fletcher, Alan Lilley, J.K. Lever and Brian Hardie (not a bad second XI) that Hussain should not be rushed. Yet he is the same age as Hutton and Compton were when they got Test hundreds at Trent Bridge against Australia in 1938.

It is interesting, incidentally, that the Essex seconds should be staying at one of the plusher hotels around Nottingham. So much for the tough life of the impecunious player on the fringe of the county side! Mind you, it is *not* an easy life. There are two young men, Nick Knight and Adam Seymour, who are both full of runs at the moment, but there is no place for them in the first team and no-one can be sure whether they will go on to greater fame or fade from the scene after a few frustrating and disappointing seasons, as many young hopefuls inevitably do.

Thursday, August 10th

Once again, Australia have total control of the Test at the end of the opening day. Border won the toss and batted on a slow pitch of true bounce and Mark Taylor and Geoff Marsh batted for six hours without being parted, the first time this has happened in a Test in England and only the ninth time in Test history. Taylor has been a revelation on this tour and he is being fairly spoken of as the new Arthur Morris. Marsh is liked and respected by everyone and it was good to see so dogged a performer making his first hundred of the series.

He was lucky not to be given out lbw to Malcolm in the first hour and the luck did go Australia's way, as it always tends to do for the superior side. A couple of chances might have been caught, but generally it was a dedicated and worthy piece of batting by both men. Malcolm looked a little lost, but not out of his depth, on his first appearance and he will do better on quicker pitches. Fraser again looked much the best bowler, though. Cook and Hemmings both bowled very tidily and Botham did too but it was on pitches such as these that he once used to beat something extra out of the

wicket through his great strength and spirit. Not, alas, any more.

I 'hosted' a dinner evening for my *TMS* colleagues Brian Johnston, Fred Trueman and Trevor Bailey whilst we tackled the enjoyable business of choosing an England Under 24 team to go on an imaginary tour of the West Indies, a competition we have been running in *The Cricketer* this summer. Finding batsmen of the right quality was easy, fast bowlers not so simple, spinners practically impossible.

Friday, August 11th

Australia went from 301 for no wicket to 560 for five. 'We didn't do badly did we?' asked the irrepressible Jack Russell in the Cornhill hospitality tent this evening and I entirely agree. Taylor made a marvellous 219, Marsh, who never got going today, 138, Boon, full of good shots, 73, Jones 22 and Border 46 not out. Nick Cook bowled well again and got some turn to take the first three wickets, two of them to stumpings, the second of them a beauty by the man who, had he played in the golden age, would no doubt have been known as the 'Stroud Stumper'. It was a particularly good one because the ball bounced shoulder-high as well as turned. I can think of one or two recent England 'keepers who would not have made it. After tea Botham had a chance for a slip catch: it flew fast to his left after a late decision by Boon to play at a ball from Malcolm. In almost making a fine catch, he severely dislocated the second finger of his right hand. When you are down in cricket you really are down.

Tuesday, August 15th

Time to reflect today on the fifth Test, which Australia duly won yesterday by an innings and 180 runs, despite a promising 47 by Michael

Atherton. Alderman, Lawson, Hughes and Hohns all did more than well. No-one expected us to win but it was deeply disappointing to spend over seven hours seeing the bowlers striving to take the first wicket of the match and then to witness Australia's easiest ever victory in England.

The one consolation is that the banality of the bowling and the technical and mental inadequacy of the batting may have been enough to convince the TCCB policy makers that enough is enough. At a dinner to launch a Richie Benaud video marking his 25 years of commentary for the BBC (he originally did a BBC training course as a young cricketer in 1956 and actually did some sound commentary in England in 1960), I was encouraged to discover that soon after a thunderstorm broke around the celebrations in the Australian dressing-room at Trent Bridge, A.C. Smith, the Board's Chief Executive, was holding a meeting with Ted Dexter and Micky Stewart during which it was decided to take the Palmer Committee's report down from the shelves, dust it off and send it round the 17 counties for further debates.

What may emerge by the end of this winter is not an exact application of the Palmer proposals, made three years ago following England's original five-nil defeat by the West Indies, but the abandonment of the 40-over Sunday League from 1991 and the adoption of a 16-match four-day County Championship. If there is one thing above all others which has led to England's current plight it is the poverty of too many pitches. The hope is that four-day cricket would force the counties to produce pitches that will last so that treasurers can recoup some of the money that would be lost from the Sunday League. Persuading local firms to buy hospitality boxes for at least the third day of every county match will be crucial to the solvency of the county game in any new structure designed to cater better than the present one for the needs of the England team. It should be possible to fit Test matches round the four-day Championship so that England players miss less Championship cricket than they do at present. These are all formidable problems which have to be tackled immediately. County members, especially those who live far from the main county grounds, will be disappointed to lose a few days of cricket watching but they too must realise that the present slide

into cricketing obscurity cannot continue.
In the end, if these changes come about, the Australians may be seen to have done us a great favour this summer. The difference between the two sides has been in technique and attitude, not talent. At Trent Bridge Australia's four bowlers, Alderman, Lawson, Hughes and Hohns, using occasional assistance from a wearing pitch, performed outstandingly in dismissing England twice in 74 fewer overs than Australia's own, voluntarily declared first innings. They built their latest victory, the fifth in their last six Tests, on the record-breaking opening stand between Geoff Marsh and the remarkable Mark Taylor. The batsmen who followed pressed home the advantage remorselessly: all of the top six in the Australian order have now scored over 300 runs in the series and Taylor, with 720, now stands second only to Bradman in the list of highest series aggregates against England, with the power to add to this total. David Gower, who scored 732 in 1985, knows how he feels.

Wednesday, August 16th

A great game of limited-overs cricket at Southampton today ended with Malcolm Marshall needing six off the last ball from Angus Fraser to take Hampshire, rather than Middlesex, to Lord's on September 2. He could not manage it. Had Chris Smith not sustained a broken thumb a quarter of an hour earlier, however, Hampshire could well have got the 268 they needed after John Carr and Desmond Haynes had both made 80s in a commanding opening stand on a beautiful wicket. Smith made 114 but

Emburey again had a say in the result when he bowled 'Kippy's' brother Robin at a point when he looked in formidable form.

Hampshire have two nuggets in the Smith brothers. They are wholly dedicated to the county and both fine batsmen. Chris, who always reminds me of Cyril Washbrook, is underestimated. He and his brother have won the Man of the Match award in all four of Hampshire's matches this season in the NatWest.

One of Middlesex's unsung players, Simon Hughes, was the eventual key to their success today, only four runs coming from his last over. He twice took wickets with his slower ball, which is really one of the best in the business. He was one of several players with whom I had a quick drink in a marquee on the side of the ground after the game. It would be rather sad if Hampshire's plans to develop a completely new cricketing centre were to come to fruition at the expense of Northlands Road just when their groundsman, Tom Flintoft, has got the square in really good condition. It is so good to hear of a ground where pitches have been consistently good, with some pace and even bounce. I always enjoy the intimate atmosphere of this ground, too and the pavilion with its graceful arches and mellow tile roof is as attractive as any in the land, remarkably similar to the one at Canterbury, another ground where the crowd feel part of the game and seem all the friendlier as a result.

I cannot be so complimentary about the commentary box at Southampton. It is a wooden hut on stilts which on days like today, is shared by Radio Solent and ourselves. Twelve people crowded into the space of about four square feet for the eight hours of this exciting match and I had a headache long before the end, partly no doubt from striking my head incessantly against the sloping ceiling!

Our summarisers today were John Barclay, who has just become a father again and has called his son Theodore (who also inherits his own third name, Troutbeck) and Vic Marks, who told me quietly that he is retiring from cricket at the end of the season to take up Scyld Berry's old job as cricket correspondent of *The Observer*.

Sunday, August 20th

I commented on the latest and last Test team of the summer this morning before returning home for a lunch party. Two uncapped players, John Stephenson and Nasser Hussain, both of Durham University and Essex, are in the 13 and if both should play along with the recalled David Capel and Gladstone Small, England will have had 30 different players in six Tests, equalling the record number in 1921. Yet perhaps as many as 15 other players could measure their records against those chosen and ask 'Why him and not me?' Amongst the batsmen, for example, Bailey, Fairbrother, Whitaker, Morris, Mendis, Nicholas, Roebuck and Benson: amongst the bowlers Cowans, Bicknell, Watkin, Childs, Thomas and DeFreitas.

'THE RACECOURSE GROUND, DURHAM UNIVERSITY'.

© JACK RUSSELL '89

Of the 12 assembled at Trent Bridge, Curtis, Moxon, Thomas and the injured Botham are missing this time. The attack is the one originally chosen for the fifth Test with Capel deservedly taking over as the all-rounder from Botham. A good performance from Capel this time is vital to his future. Devon Malcolm had back spasms yesterday and may have to withdraw. It is a pity no gamble has been taken with Medlycott. It would be a major surprise to see Cook and Hemmings bowling England to a Test victory, especially so in England.

It is likely that Hemmings or Small will be 12th man with either Stephenson - if Gower chooses to open - or Hussain also dropping out. The alternative is to play all the batsmen and only three specialist bowlers since Capel, Gooch, Atherton and Stephenson can all bowl.

If Hussain plays, his first Test will be only his 24th first-class match

at the age of 21. He is widely recognised, however, as a batsman of the highest class and there is every reason to promote him now, provided he is given time to settle.

Stephenson is a hard-hitting opener of the modern school who has only established himself fully in the Essex side this season after an outstanding schoolboy career at Felstead – the school Derek Pringle also went to – and, ironically, a successful winter in South Africa. His hundred in Holland last week clearly impressed Micky Stewart.

He must be considered a bit lucky to displace Moxon, who got two near-unplayable balls at Trent Bridge and whose technique looks sounder than Curtis's although Ted Dexter went out of his way to say today that Curtis would not be forgotten.

Gooch's return has to be welcomed in that he is the best English batsman after Gatting, but I feel uneasy about the way that he was allowed to take a quick sabbatical with Essex even if the suggestion initially came from the manager, Micky Stewart. Australians would say, probably rightly, that he should either be wholeheartedly committed to England or not play at all.

Tuesday, August 22nd

Yet another day of frantic activity for the England manager Micky Stewart began with the shattering news that Angus Fraser, the only reliable fast bowler in the last three Tests, had twisted his knee again. Greg Thomas was immediately contacted when Angus Fraser dropped out yesterday, but told Stewart that he had already decided, partly because he was left out in the first place, to accept the offer to join the unofficial England tour of South Africa. He had told Stewart in Holland last week that the offer had been made and he decided, probably only in the last few days, that his career as a Test player was too uncertain for him to turn it down. So another talented cricketer is lost from the dwindling pool of available players.

Even as an alternative was being sought, Laurie Brown, the England physiotherapist, phoned Lord's to say that Philip DeFreitas would have to be ruled out with a damaged hamstring only 24 hours after his call-up as a replacement for Devon Malcolm. This left Stewart and Dexter to discuss with David Gower when he came off the field after a tense battle with Surrey to consider a list headed by the country's two leading wicket-takers, Derek Pringle and Steve Watkin, followed by Jon Agnew, Simon Base, Martin Bicknell, Adrian Jones, Alan Igglesden and Neil Williams. Norman Cowans and Ricardo Ellcock were apparently out of contention because of injury.

It is uncanny, not to say bizarre, how every England team of the series, bar none, has been affected by injuries to key players shortly before the match. One may not have agreed with all the original selections made by Ted Dexter, Micky Stewart and David Gower but criticism of them has to be tempered with sympathy for the extraordinary run of bad luck. Old pros will be shaking their heads this evening and wondering how it is that with all their muscle-stretching today's fast bowlers seem so desperately injury-prone. Not enough bowling in the middle, too many physical jerks, some of them will say. But the West Indian fast bowlers do more exercising than the rest and most of them keep fit. Is it more because English players simply lack strength, enjoying too soft a life from their schooldays upwards?

Wednesday, August 23rd

Up to London for my Test previews. The two replacements with whom the selectors eventually emerged were faithful old 'Pring' from Essex and Kent's Alan Igglesden, a complete unknown to most people. He is tall with a high action and has done an honest if unspectacular season's work for a struggling team. The inside word was that Gower wanted Jon Agnew but the other two selectors obviously felt they must answer the public call for fresh young faces. I did a brief interview with Igglesden, who was obviously delighted and surprised by his sudden rise to fame. I am sure he and John Stephenson are both aware that more than one player in recent years has appeared in an Oval Test and has never been seen for England again. Those that come to mind are Paul Parker, Alan Butcher and Rob Bailey. Bailey has been especially unlucky not to get another chance. As for the other two, Butcher is now Glamorgan captain and was the first England-qualified player to reach 1000 runs this year and Parker has done a great job in galvanising the drifting and demoralised Sussex side of two years ago.

Thursday, August 24th

We had the traditional *Test Match Special* dinner at Broadcasting House this evening, kindly given by the BBC as a 'thank you' to the commentators and also to entertain some of our friends from MCC and TCCB. The delightfully affable MCC Secretary John Stephenson handed Brian Johnston a letter tonight which informed him that the Committee had resolved to make him a life member of the club; that gave us all pleasure. It was also within a day of the anniversary of Fred Trueman's immortal 300th Test wicket, that of Neil Hawke at The Oval in 1964. Peter Baxter had arrived with John Arlott's brilliant description of the event which was played prior to a presentation to the great man. The special touch in Arlott's commentary of what happened immediately Cowdrey took the catch at slip was 'And Trueman congratulates Hawke' (not the other way round!).

Pat Ewing, head of Radio Five, which is scheduled to start in September next year, was reassuring about her undoubted commitment to *TMS* and would obviously prefer that we should not be interrupted at all from our day-long chatter, come rain or shine. It remains to be seen, however, whether anyone will be able to find another network to switch our commentary to when we clash with other major sporting events like Wimbledon, umpteen race meetings and the interminable major soccer matches. I very much fear we shall never be quite the same.

Once again I stayed the night with the Johnstons in St John's Wood to save me a late journey tonight and an early one tomorrow to beat the rush hour.

Friday, August 25th

England, having had the misfortune to lose the toss yesterday, inevitably had to chase leather again all day as Taylor, Boon, Border and, especially, Jones enjoyed themselves on a beautiful pitch. But then they actually took four wickets this morning and had Australia all out for a mere four by mid afternoon. Jones had scored a really brilliant hundred yesterday but it was cloudy and humid this morning and no batsman was at ease. Pringle took the last four wickets - welcome success for a very good cricketer and likeable man-before, incredibly, Alderman had Gooch lbw yet again with the third ball of the innings. It was the fifth time in the series that Alderman had got a wicket in his first over. No wonder England have been beaten. You must have successful opening bowlers and opening batsmen to win Test series and in Alderman and Taylor Australia have had both.

Soon after Gooch was out it rained and we commentators were obliged to earn our corn by chatting on and on until play was eventually called off after six o'clock. Dicky Bird joined us at one point and began telling cricket stories with tremendous gusto apparently unaware that he was on air.

Duty done, I went across London to Lord's to attend the eve of Village Championship Final dinner. This is always a delightful occasion with two genuine village teams thrilled beyond description at earning the right to play at Lord's after a season of tense, combative cricket and many extraordinary individual deeds. Wives and girlfriends are present too, relishing the free night at the Hilton Hotel and getting their reward for loyal support of their cricket-mad loved ones, not to mention their inevitable assistance with the teas.

This was the last year of the sponsorship of Hydro Fertilisers whose executive all say that they have got genuine value for money from patronising the competition, which *The Cricketer* magazine has run since its inception. We are a little worried that no company has stepped into the breach and a little baffled, too, because this year, with Hambledon, the most famous village of them all, reaching the final against Toft from Cheshire, publicity has been greater than ever. There was even a Bavarian television crew filing into dinner this evening. Goodness knows what they will make of it, or of the final tomorrow, when coachloads of supporters will be up to support both villages and the boxes on the Tavern side will all be full. Hambledon is expected to be deserted and it is rather unfortunate that the final clashes with the annual village flower show!

Mark Nicholas was the very appropriate and amusing guest speaker this evening and he made special mention of Hambledon's 48 year old off-spinner 'Topsy' Turner, whose bowling helped win the semi-final and whose son is a promising young left-arm spinner on the Hampshire staff.

Saturday, August 26th

Robin M-J and Philip Hudson, who have had very successful seasons for both their Horsham and their Sussex age-groups (Robin once getting three hundreds in successive 20 over matches, though the bowling was, he said, poor), came up to The Oval today but unfortunately saw England being outplayed again, on another cloudy day which eventually dissolved into rain with England struggling desperately at 124 for six. Gower was at his best in making 43 not out and John Stephenson's start in Test cricket was full of merit in that he played with confidence and a straight bat before becoming one of four more victims for Alderman, the smiling assassin.

Sunday, August 27th

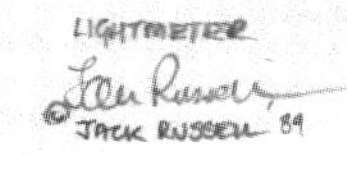

After three days of Test cricket and two dinners I was glad of a day at home today although only partially so because after church it was off to Albury to lead my team of 'celebrities' into friendly battle against the England Ladies in aid of the Albury Recreational Trust and Cherry Trees, the home for mentally handicapped children at East Clandon, the second of the three villages in which we have lived.

We had a similar match two years ago when I had raised a side, but this year the voluntary workers at Cherry Trees and the Albury club members had done all the work and done it marvellously, Chris Cain being the organising genius. There was a large, enthusiastic crowd and ample entertainment for them on the fringes of that lovely, heathland ground, lest they should get bored by the spectacle of unfit television presenters being taught the art of cricket by the girls!

Megan Lear, Barbara Daniels, Janette Brittin, Sarah Potter, Jill McConway and company all played delightful cricket and Janet Aspinall hit the winning runs off a long-hop from myself with one over left! Over £5000 was the estimate of the money raised: well worthwhile. Amongst those who stood out for my eleven were Rory Bremner and John Kettley, both great characters and genuinely useful cricketers, the British Olympic hockey captain, Richard Dodds, who played a fine innings, and the two

Spurs footballers, David Howells and Paul 'Gazza' Gascoigne, who kept wicket better than he batted. Out first ball!

Monday, August 28th

A sunnier day today helped England to avoid the follow-on with a delightful 79 from Gower and staunch tailend performances by Small, Pringle and Cook. The wicket remains very good and England should now escape with a draw.

Wednesday, August 30th

The Test series is over and there is a brief respite before the climax of the county programme. I am sure I was not alone in feeling a sense of deep relief last night when I got in the car at eight o'clock at Archbishop's Tennison's Grammar School and drove away from The Oval, the great, dirty metropolitan ground already enveloped by an autumnal dusk. Summer after summer one looks forward to the cricket season and it flies by all too quickly, too intensely, so that one event runs into another and savouring the great moments is almost impossible. Perhaps that is what memory is for. I had a desperately busy end to the match, having to reel off news reports and summaries of the series, not to mention prognostications for the future, in one commentary box, in between dashing next door to the Radio Three box to help to keep the chat going until all the presentations and the farewells had been made.

We were able to present David Gower with a consolation magnum of champagne, reward for the brilliant left-handed slip catch in the Australian first innings which we commentators, acting as judges on behalf of the Savoy, who have been celebrating their centenary, had decided was the 'champagne moment' of the match. We were all glad to be able to give David something because he has had a deeply disappointing season culminating in a characteristically loose stroke as England were supposed to be fighting for a draw. They managed it with the help of an over-cautious declaration by Border and some bad light as the game ended in anti-climax; but, of course, almost all the champagne moments throughout the series have belonged to Australia.

The sunny weather, the fact that all their men remained fit and the extraordinary bad luck which afflicted England from the moment that Gatting and Botham had to drop out of the first Test, all conspired in Australia's favour, but they have richly deserved their success for all that. The sheer quality and determination of their cricket has been the essential reason for winning the series four-nil, earning legitimate comparisons with the best Australian sides of the past.

Australia beat England three-nil in 1921, having crushed them five-nil at home only a few months before. Indeed Armstrong's team travelled to England on the same ship as the beaten touring side. At least England then managed draws in the last two Tests. In 1948 they managed only one draw, at Old Trafford, where they actually had the best of it and forced Bradman and Morris to fight for survival on the last day. Otherwise Australian domination, 41 years on, has been as great as it was in Bradman's day.

Against the counties the Australians had eight wins, five draws and one defeat, against Worcestershire in May, while they were still finding their feet. Two one-day defeats, against Sussex and to England in the first of the Texaco games, were their only other reverses.

Thursday, August 31st

While Worcestershire were nipping in very unexpectedly and winning the Championship, I was innocently engaged in my first game for Horsham today since breaking my thumb. Against the Horsham Under 19s I holed out for a duck, took no wickets and damaged a finger dropping a devilishly hard catch on the square-leg boundary! The Colts won, for the first time in the living memory of all except the remarkable Doctor Dew, thanks to a marvellously confident century by Ralph Olliphant-Cullum who is captain of Brighton College and an outstanding magician as well as sportsman. Rodney, his proud father, was umpiring and soon got the better of a swift exchange of views with Horsham's witty but occasionally over-loquacious captain 'Doughy' Baker!

Although there was no way that I could have 'covered' the match, which started on the Tuesday during the Test match, I still felt a little guilty and deprived this evening when I got home to find that Worcestershire had beaten Gloucestershire in three days at New Road to regain their Britannic Assurance Championship title. Last year I had seen them win back the pennant amid scenes of great joy after another three-day victory so I could imagine the scenario this year.

Who can say Worcestershire's triumph has not been well earned when so many of their 'star' players have been injured so often? Into the boots of Dilley, Botham and Newport stepped two enthusiastic young medium fast bowlers, Steve McKewan and Stewart Lampitt, both of whom got their caps today as I heard from Mike Vockins when I rang the club on getting back home.

He also told me that my invitation for an autumn visit to see the cricket scene in Zimbabwe has been withdrawn because a 'Triple-Wicket' tournament there has had to be cancelled. John Hick, the organiser, had not been in touch so it was as well that I heard at second hand. Much rearranging now becomes necessary.

SEPTEMBER

Friday, September 1st

I previewed the NatWest Final en route to Copdock in Suffolk for the 150th anniversary dinner of a flourishing club. The folk of Essex and Suffolk had some very uncomplimentary things to say about the powers-that-be in English cricket. They seem to think Dexter a disaster and, moreover, that Essex have been robbed of the Championship by the Southend pitch decision. Such comments are usually prefaced, however, by 'I dare say I'm biased but...' Rural England would not be England if there were not plenty of people willing to have a hearty moan about the establishment, but cricket club dinners are a very useful gauge to me about how people are thinking.

Saturday, September 2nd

Having been 'deprived' of the eight days of Championship cricket with which I usually finish the first-class season, the NatWest Final instead marked the climax.

As usual there was a tremendous sense of occasion, with Lord's packed. This time next year its capacity will substantially have risen by means of the extended Compton and Edrich Stands at the Nursery End. Happily, although it was cool all day, the weather was fine and the pitch was dry enough for Mike Gatting to choose to bat first when he won the toss for Middlesex.

In the event the pitch was a bit too slow for there to be any dazzling strokeplay and for much of the day the bowlers of both sides were on top.

Happily, Angus Fraser looked the best of the lot, although I hope Norman Cowans impressed the selectors enough to realise that they have been unwise to undervalue his accuracy.

As Warwickshire's reply developed in fits and starts, it seemed that Middlesex had a hold on the game, albeit a tenuous one, but these games have a history of dramatic finishes in the twilight and this was no exception. Dermot Reeve, man of the match for

Sussex a few years back, added a shrewd, competitive innings to his good spell of bowling, and brought the team within range before being deftly run-out by a combination of Haynes and Emburey. At the crunch Neil Smith, the broad-shouldered and bespectacled son of his famous father M.J.K., walked out into the gloom and crashed the second ball of the final over from Hughes far over long-off for the six which effectively won the game.

Monday, September 4th

Who is going to captain England in the winter is the question being asked in every newspaper today.

Although Ted Dexter and David Gower spoke to each other on Friday, there will be no final decision until tomorrow afternoon when Ted Dexter, Micky Stewart, Ossie Wheatley and A.C. Smith, the full England committee, meet at Lord's. They have to decide whom to invite to lead England on the three winter tours – the short one to India for a one-day tournament, the important A tour to Zimbabwe after Christmas and the simultaneous 'mission impossible' to the West Indies starting at the end of January. Once decided, the captains will be announced at 10.00 on Thursday morning and will spend most of the rest of the day with the selectors helping to choose the teams which will be announced at the same time on Friday.

It will be a major surprise if Gower is reappointed, although the weekend 'revelations', were ambiguous. It's pretty obvious England need a change of direction, and that could in theory be provided by Gower himself. But that is, of course, unlikely. It would require almost blind faith to appoint the man who has just led England to a four-nil defeat by Australia and whose last ten Tests in charge against the West Indies all ended in defeat. On the other hand no-one expects England to win this time. A captain with experience and worth his place in the team is essential.

Of the alternatives Gooch, despite a run of failures since the second Test at Lord's, 0, 8,11,13, 0,10 -42 in six innings, is the most likely choice of a committee whose inclinations are conservative. Despite India last year, I understand from West Indian cricketing sources that there would be no political objections to him and at his best Gooch remains the only England opening batsman about whom the West Indies fast bowlers might lose even a wink of sleep. Lamb, Botham and Willey can probably be discounted.

Personally I would look outside the group of established Test cricketers. Parker, Nicholas, Roebuck, Neale and Greig all have qualities which fit them for the job. Roebuck probably comes nearest to being worth a place as a player alone. Parker (the rank outsider) would be my own choice for his ability to galvanise a team in the field.

Wednesday, September 6th

The more prosaic business of county cricket carried on today and so too does the incredible weather. I drove up to Manchester last night past fields totally devoid of moisture with sheep nibbling hopefully at pasture the colour of white straw. Some of the scenes could easily have come from Australia: our green and pleasant land has become a parched and thirsty one.

Today's business was the semi-final of the Refuge Assurance Cup, a spurious addition to the Sunday League which nevertheless attracted a largish crowd at Old Trafford. Nottinghamshire won by five wickets in the last of their 40 overs against Lancashire, who had won the League itself, but whose fielding today was not up to scratch. Randall, by contrast, was at his sparkling, marvellously eccentric best.

In the other game Worcestershire were soundly beaten at home by Essex who are desperately keen to win something after losing their pacemaking positions in the Britannic Championship and the Sunday League, not to mention losing the B and H to Notts off the last ball. They have their chance of revenge now and there will no doubt be a full house at Edgbaston on Sunday week.

Forty over cricket may not do the players any good but it has many advantages for spectators and, having enjoyed one of my occasional days in a TV, as opposed to radio, box, I was away from the ground at six, at least an hour and a half earlier than usual, with the sun still shining and Dvorak on the cassette player to ease the long motorway grind.

Thursday, September 7th

The first of two days at Lord's for me and two days of decision for the England Committee. Shortly before one o'clock I was told by Peter Smith, the TCCB's always helpful Press Officer (formerly *Daily Mail* Cricket Correspondent – poacher turned gamekeeper?) that the new England captain was, so to speak, an old one: Graham Gooch. The immediate question from James Naughtie on *The World at One* was, of course, what would be the reaction of the Indian and Caribbean Governments? The answer was that much has changed since the Indians refused Gooch a visa when he was appointed captain for the winter tour at the same time last year. This time it suits the Prime Minister to be holding a prestigious (though that is a matter of opinion, I think it is spurious) One-Day international tournament shortly before an Election, so there will be no problem for Gooch now. (Nor will there be, I would bet any money, for the six senior Indian players who have been banned by their Board for playing in North America without their sanction; it is an entirely safe prediction that they will be pardoned.) As for the West Indies, no doubt there will be some contacts with South Africa, but the Caricom Prime Ministers have pledged support for the ICC Concordat so, for better or worse, the tour will go ahead.

I would have preferred a more adventurous choice as captain, but Gooch has obvious virtues, not the least being that he must still be, against a West Indies attack anyway, a certain choice to open the innings. He is also a good, solid, likeable character, with a sense of humour which seldom comes across from the field of play, and he is thoroughly dedicated to his profession. He will spread the feeling, not inappropriately in present circumstances, that nothing worthwhile comes without hard work. In all these respects he has much in common with Allan Border. Like Border, too, he must have learned a good deal about tactics from England's captain *manqué*, Keith Fletcher.

Ted Dexter said that no fewer than 12 candidates were discussed, including, presumably, Gower, Botham, Greig, Roebuck, Parker, Nicholas and Neale.

This afternoon Gooch sat down with Dexter, Stewart, Wheatley and A.C. Smith to decide who would go on the three winter tours. Just for fun, these are the teams I guess they will announce at 10.00 at Lord's tomorrow:

To West Indies: Gooch, Mendis, Benson, Smith, R.A., Lamb, Bailey, Gower, Stewart, Capel, Russell, Childs, Hemmings, Fraser, Cowans, Small, Lawrence, Ellcock.

To Zimbabwe: Nicholas, Stephenson, Bicknell D., Blakey, Hussain, Atherton, Fairbrother, Pringle, Lewis C., Rhodes, Medlycott, Afford, Bicknell M., Igglesden, A. Malcolm, Watkin.

Friday, September 8th

I cheated a bit yesterday by putting 17 in the West Indies team and 16 in the one to Zimbabwe. In each case there will be one player fewer although I think there was a strong case for taking 17 to the West Indies rather than flying out a replacement when the inevitable injuries occur. I was wrong about Benson and Mendis and horribly wrong about Gower. They are taking Wayne Larkins as the only opener apart from Gooch and there is no left-hander in the entire party to the West Indies. Larkins is a fine player of fast bowing, without doubt, and perhaps he will prove an inspired selection but the odds must be against it. If the team is short of grafters, it is also short of reliably accurate fast bowlers. The actual side is:

Gooch, Larkins, Lamb (vice captain), Smith, Bailey, Hussain, Stewart, Capel, Russell, Hemmings, Medlycott, Fraser, Small, Malcolm, Ellcock, De Freitas.

The vast majority of press questions to Ted Dexter when the team was announced in the Lord's Banqueting Suite before a battery of cameras concerned the unfortunate Gower and Botham. The only question mark about David in my mind was whether, deep down, he really wants another tour of the West Indies. On his batting record there, he deserved to go. Sadly, the same cannot be said of Ian. It is illogical that Hussain has been preferred to Atherton when the reverse was true against Australia but the latter is to be vice-captain in Zimbabwe so he is rightly being given a chance to show that he could be a long-term England captain. Stewart could well get in the side as a batsman. There are any number of disappointed men around the country this evening who have no place on either tour: they include Gower, Botham, Lawrence, Cowans, Agnew, Mendis, Ramprakash, Fairbrother, John Morris, Benson, Curtis, Moxon, and Roebuck – whose hopes were rather unfairly raised by the fact that he was made captain of the trip to Holland, where his articulacy with the press probably frightened off the powers-that-be. If so, what a reflection on those powers! Nick Cook goes to India only.

The side going to Zimbabwe is: Nicholas, captain; Atherton, vice-captain; Darren Bicknell, Stephenson, Blakey, Whitaker, Thorpe, Lewis, Pringle, Afford, Illingworth, Rhodes, Igglesden, Martin Bicknell, Watkin.

Under the genial Nicholas I am sure they will enjoy themselves and do well.

Saturday, September 16th

We have had so many exciting finishes to the County Championship since Britannic Assurance took over as sponsors that it was inevitable that sooner or later the season would disappear with a whimper instead of a bang, although the final curtain on the county season will not go down until tomorrow night when Essex and Nottinghamshire will have battled it out at Edgbaston for the last prize of the season, the Refuge Assurance Final. What will be the overwhelming feeling when I turn the car southwards for the last of the season's many motorway marathons? Well the sorrow that it is over will be mixed with relief that a season which promised such an exciting, elevated struggle for the Ashes turned out to be, instead, a match between a battleship and a leaking sailing boat. Captain Gower's ship soon sunk and if there weren't red faces at The Admiralty there ought to have been.

The saddest comment I heard all season was from one of the England cricketers who *didn't* get chosen this season: 'I thought things would change for the better with Ted Dexter, but nothing *has* changed.' The best one can say in the First Sea Lord's defence is: give him a bit more time.

Even if Essex win tomorrow's relatively modest prize of £5,250, all connected with the club feel deprived by the fact that Worcestershire and not Essex will forever be inscribed in the books of record as the 1989 County Champions.

The fact is that Worcestershire are not unworthy Champions. Despite injuries to their three most experienced fast bowlers, Dilley, Botham and Pridgeon, and the long absence of that prolific wicket-taker Philip Newport through an achilles tendon injury, they found two young bowlers with fire in their bellies in Steve McEwan and Stuart Lampitt who were both awarded county caps on the day that Worcestershire nipped in to retain their title by beating Gloucestershire on the third evening of a four-day game.

If Essex were the nearly team of 1989 they must still be deemed to have had a successful season and the Southend blemish apart – a problem, after all, not entirely in their own control – they still finished second in the Championship and were beaten off only the final ball by Nottinghamshire in a wonderful finish to the Benson and Hedges Cup Final.

That golden evening at Lord's is a reminder that the happiest aspect of the 1989 season was the quite wonderfully sunny weather. Only three have compared with it since the War – 1947, 1959 and 1976. Bowlers especially found it hard work, despite the dreadful state of too many of our county pitches, which makes it odd that the leading wicket-taker, Steve Watkin, should have played for the bottom club, Glamorgan. No one-season wonder he.

Third place in the main table was always going to go to Middlesex or Lancashire but Middlesex had the NatWest Trophy stolen from them by Warwickshire in another thrilling finish at Lord's, whereas Lancashire won the Sunday League before one of those immense and excited crowds who used to pack Old Trafford in the early days of the competition.

Warwickshire's form in the second half of the season was in direct contrast to that of Northamptonshire, the season's most serious under-achievers. Even with Allan Lamb injured for so long a side containing Geoff Cook, Larkins, Bailey, Capel, Greg Thomas, Ambrose or Winston Davis and Nick Cook, with Dennis Lillee even signed on for some coaching, really should have won something. Perhaps they should take a lesson from Essex and Worcestershire in the art of man management.

Kent, Surrey, Gloucestershire, Yorkshire and Leicestershire were other counties whose early hopes came to nothing and not all of them had the sort of consolation Surrey had when four of their young players were selected for winter tours.

LEICESTERSHIRE FOX
© JACK RUSSELL '89

No such luck for Sussex, despite the steady improvement evident throughout a season of positive cricket or for Yorkshire who have only one player going on either tour and whose members will either have to swallow their pride and accept an overseas player or resign themselves to further barren seasons.

Amongst the individuals who will look back on the county season with special pride are Watkin, Angus Fraser, Derek Pringle and Franklyn Stephenson – all bowlers – and Alan Wells as the most unsung of the free-scoring batsmen. One man stood supreme, however: Jimmy Cook, the South African schoolmaster, who, like the Australians, taught all the British players around him that a good basic technique, along with courage and commitment, is the time-honoured way to success in cricket.

As always at the end of a season there are some sad farewells, most notably this time to three justly popular men, Jack Simmons, Vic Marks and John Lever, who shared some of the same qualities, not least a profound respect for the game and a worthy pride in their team's and their own performances.

Sunday, September 17th

Well, there was a happy ending for John Lever. He could not actually play in the Refuge Assurance Final at Edgbaston, because of a bad back, but at least Essex won. They did so only, however, after a most exciting finish, this time when Eddie Hemmings concluded a low-scoring match on a spinners' pitch by lofting Derek Pringle high to long-on. It was the fourth ball of the final over and had he hit it a few yards further and flatter it would have been the six which won the match for Nottinghamshire. Such little margins sometimes separate success from failure in cricket, as in life. My own season starts afresh now. Before the end of the month I have six matches lined up, three for Horsham and three for The Cross Arrows at Lord's. It can't rain in them all – not in 1989!